Loveability

Love·a·bil·it·y / ˈlʌvəbiliti / *noun*

♥ Also by Robert Holden, Ph.D. ♥

Books

Happiness NOW!

Authentic Success (formerly titled *Success Intelligence*)

Be Happy

Shift Happens!

CD Programs

Be Happy

Follow Your Joy

Happiness NOW!

Shift Happens!

Success Intelligence

Flip Calendars

Happiness NOW!

Success NOW!

All of the above are available at your local bookstore,
or may be ordered by visiting:

Hay House USA: **www.hayhouse.com**®
Hay House Australia: **www.hayhouse.com.au**
Hay House UK: **www.hayhouse.co.uk**
Hay House South Africa: **www.hayhouse.co.za**
Hay House India: **www.hayhouse.co.in**

Loveability

Love·a·bil·it·y / ˈluvəbiliti / *noun*

Knowing How to Love and Be Loved

Robert Holden, Ph.D.

HAY HOUSE, INC.
Carlsbad, California • New York City
London • Sydney • Johannesburg
Vancouver • Hong Kong • New Delhi

Published and distributed in the United States by: Hay House, Inc.: www .hayhouse.com® • **Published and distributed in Australia by:** Hay House Australia Pty. Ltd.: www.hayhouse.com.au • **Published and distributed in the United Kingdom by:** Hay House UK, Ltd.: www.hayhouse.co.uk • **Published and distributed in the Republic of South Africa by:** Hay House SA (Pty), Ltd.: www.hayhouse. co.za • **Distributed in Canada by:** Raincoast: www.raincoast.com • **Published in India by:** Hay House Publishers India: www.hayhouse.co.in

Cover design: Celia Fuller-Vels and Karla Baker • *Interior design:* Tricia Breidenthal

"Late Fragment" from *A New Path to the Waterfall,* copyright © 1989 by the Estate of Raymond Carver. Used by permission of Grove/Atlantic, Inc. Any third party use of this material, outside of this publication, is prohibited.

"The Sun Never Says," from *The Gift,* © 1999. Used by permission of Daniel Ladinsky.

"It Happens All the Time in Heaven," from *The Subject Tonight Is Love: 60 Wild and Sweet Poems of Hafiz,* © 1996. Used by permission of Daniel Ladinsky.

"I Know the Way You Can Get," from *I Heard God Laughing,* © 1996. Used by permission of Daniel Ladinsky.

"Only Love Can Explain Love," from *Teachings of Rumi,* by Andrew Harvey, © 1999. Used by permission of the publisher.

Library of Congress Cataloging-in-Publication Data

Holden, Robert
  Loveability* : *love-a-bil-it-y/'luv[?]biliti/noun learning how to love and be loved / Robert Holden, Ph.D. -- 1st edition.
       pages cm
  On the title page "[?]" appears as the phonetic schwa (upside-down e) symbol.
  Includes bibliographical references.
  ISBN 978-1-4019-4162-8 (hardcover : alk. paper) 1. Love. 2. Interpersonal relations. I. Title.
  BF575.L8H644 2013
  152.4'1--dc23
                                  2012043248

Hardcover ISBN: 978-1-4019-4162-8
Digital ISBN: 978-1-4019-4164-2

16 15 14 13   4 3 2 1
1st edition, March 2013

Printed in the United States of America

♥ To Hollie, to Bo, to Christopher,
and to everyone ♥

*"If you achieve the faintest glimmering
of what love means today,
you have advanced in distance without measure
and in time beyond the count of years
to your release."*

A Course in Miracles

♥ Contents ♥

❤ Foreword ❤

Of all the things there are to learn—philosophy and mathematics, poetry and law, all the arts and all the sciences—what could be more important than that we learn how to love? If humanity knew how to love more deeply, more fundamentally and universally, how different might our world be? Would there still be war? Would there still be violence? Would there still be such unnecessary suffering within and around us?

As sophisticated as we are in our understanding of some things, we're often remedial in our ability to love. In a world where fear has a grip on human consciousness, it takes a conscious effort to take a stand against it. We yearn for love desperately, yet resist it fiercely.

Loveability is a guide to unlearning the ways of fear and choosing love instead. The task sounds simple, but it is rarely easy. Each of us has to face a lion's den of fears that lurk in the cave of our own subconscious minds, whenever we make the effort to love. And that is why we read books like this one: to have something powerful to lean on, sentences and chapters to teach us, as we make our way past our own fears to the light of love on the other side.

Robert Holden has a way with words, and, more important, he has a way with people. You feel loved in his presence; he has clearly done the inner work of moving past his own defenses, making space in his heart for someone else's love to enter. And when he does that—when any of us do that—miracles happen.

Breakthroughs occur. Insights emerge. Fears dissolve. And that is the purpose and gift of this book: like a soft and gentle massage of the heart, it breaks through barriers to our ability to love and makes room for new life to enter. That's how you'll feel when you've completed *Loveability.* Much lighter . . . more loving . . . and happier, for sure.

Marianne Williamson

♥ Introduction ♥

Imagine this.

One day, our children will learn about love at school. They will take classes in love and self-esteem, explore the meaning of "I love you," learn to listen to their hearts, and be encouraged to follow their joy. It will be normal for parents to help their children learn how to love and be loved. Adults won't be content just to read romantic novels or watch rom-com movies; they will seek out friends and lovers who are interested in real love and who want to become more loving men and women.

One day, every society on our planet will honor and celebrate the importance of love. Politics without love will be a thing of the past. Leaders who demonstrate love-based values, like service and compassion, will be elected for their vision, their courage, and their strength of character. Economists will teach the world that money does not work without love. They will offer us love-based economic policies that eradicate poverty and hunger and help us to experience real abundance and freedom.

One day, all the great professions will include love in their training syllabi and core values. Medical doctors will treat their patients with love, and psychologists will teach their patients about love. Physicists will teach us that separation is an "optical delusion" and that oneness is reality. Biologists will teach us that the survival of the species depends on cooperation, not competition. Architects and lawyers will help us to build a society on love. And ecologists will show us how to love our planet more.

One day, the major religions will recognize a God of unconditional love, and they will stop teaching people to fear God. Never again will we go to war in the name of God. Theologians and philosophers, humanists and atheists, will set aside their differences for the sake of love, and they will teach us that love is stronger than fear, that *only love is real,* and that, ultimately, love is the key to our enlightenment and evolution. And all the while, the artists of the day will serenade us and entertain us with their plays of love.

Imagine that.

That day is not here yet, I know. I believe it will come, though. Our world must evolve in the direction of love if it is to have a future. Each of us is called to do something, in the name of love, to make sure that humanity comes to understand itself and is able to choose love over fear.

The word *loveability* might be new to you. You can't find a definition for it in any standard dictionary. Not yet, anyway. Language is always evolving, as are we, and so one day you will find a dictionary that carries a definition for *loveability.* And if I am asked to help wordsmith the entry for *loveability,* I will recommend something simple like "the ability to love and be loved."

This book, *Loveability,* is a meditation on love. It addresses the most important thing you will ever learn. All the happiness, health, and abundance you experience in life comes directly from your *ability to love and be loved.* This ability is innate, not acquired. It does not need to be taught afresh, in the way you might learn some new algebra theory or memorize lines from *Romeo and Juliet.* It is a natural ability that is encoded in the essence of who you are. Any

> *"The greatest thing you'll ever learn is just to love and be loved in return."*
>
> **Eden Ahbez**

learning feels more like *remembering* something you have always known about.

Loveability is written in five parts.

In Part I, *Love Is Your Destiny,* I encourage you to explore your relationship to love and what love means to you. I ask you to consider that the goal of your life is not just to *find* love; it is to *be* love. Love is the real work of your life. It is your spiritual path. It is the key to your growth and evolution. I also assert that your destiny is not just to love one person; it is to love everyone. This is the real meaning of love. I think this is what John Lennon meant when he said:

> **It matters not who you love, where you love,**
> **why you love, when you love or how you love,**
> **it matters only that you love.**

In Part II, *Love Is Who You Are,* I help you explore the basic drama within yourself that you play out in all your relationships. This basic drama is between your Unconditioned Self (the original you) and your learned self (your self-image). The basic truth is "I am loveable" and the basic fear is "I am not loveable." Self-love is about knowing who you are. It is about identifying with love. Self-love is also about self-acceptance and giving up resistance to love. The bottom line is that *real self-love is good for you, good for your family, good for your friends, and good for the planet.*

In Part III, *Love Has No Conditions,* I share some exercises I teach in my three-day public program called Loveability. Some people think of love only as "loving others," whereas others are mostly concerned with "being loved." How about you? Of course, the art of loving must include being able *to love and be loved.* It is only when you allow yourself to

> *"To love and be loved*
> *is to feel the sun*
> *from both sides."*
>
> **David Viscott**

give and receive love freely that you realize that love is not a trade; it is a way of being.

If love is so wonderful, why does it hurt so much? And if love is meant to be so natural, why is it so difficult? And if love is meant to be so powerful, why does it not last? In Part IV, *Love Knows No Fear,* I focus on some of the common blocks to love, such as expectations and rules, independence and sacrifice, and trying to change or control each other. I also introduce you to the *True Love Checklist,* which will help you to recognize love and also to cultivate more loving relationships in your life.

In Part V, *Love Is the Answer,* I propose that *without forgiveness, you would not be able to realize your ability to love and be loved.* Forgiveness is that aspect of love that enables you to make a basic choice between love or fear, love or pain, love or guilt, and so on. Here, I also assert that love is intelligent, and that love is our true power, and that if we apply enough love to any challenge, personal or collective, we will arrive at a positive solution. *The greatest influence you can have in any situation is to be the presence of love.*

To write *Loveability,* I have drawn on a lifetime of experiences and conversations with my parents, my brother, my friends, my wife, and, more recently, my two young children. Over the years, I have engaged in dialogues on love with philosophers, biologists, priests, business leaders, physicists, and mystics. I have also been most fortunate to have had personal mentors and teachers like Tom Carpenter, Chuck Spezzano, Russ Hudson, Louise Hay, and Marianne Williamson, to name a few.

As you read *Loveability* you will notice two other big sources of inspiration. First is my work with the Loveability three-day public program. I've been teaching this program for a few years now, as well as other courses like Love and the Enneagram and also Love and Fear (based on the teachings of *A Course in Miracles*). Second, I have included several stories and conversations from my private practice with individuals and couples (names have been changed throughout to respect confidentiality).

Most of all, writing *Loveability* was inspired by what I can best describe as a process of *inner listening*. Each time I sat at my desk to write, I'd begin with a few moments of stillness and then *ask love to teach me about love*. I did this with the full awareness that I wasn't "talking" to something outside myself. This was an inner attunement. I share this so as to emphasize that loveability isn't really learned from books, public programs, or counseling sessions (as helpful as that is); it's learned by *letting the love that is your true nature teach you how to love and be loved.*

Robert Holden
London
October 2012

PART I

Love Is
Your Destiny

"I'm looking for love," said Evelyne, as she moved around in her chair, trying to get comfortable.

"How is it going?" I asked.

"Not great," she said.

"How long have you been looking?" I asked.

"About four years now," she said, trying to smile. "But it feels like a lot longer than that."

"How much longer?"

"Too long," she sighed, her eyes flitting around my office.

"That's a long time to be searching for love."

"Yes."

"Evelyne, have you ever considered giving up the search?"

"Oh, plenty of times," she laughed.

Conversations with Evelyne were full of jousting and play. She had a stoic sense of humor, which I enjoyed very much, but I chose not to laugh with her this time. What we were talking about was too precious to run away from. So I fixed my eyes on Evelyne's eyes and very deliberately asked her again, "Evelyne, have you ever thought about giving up the search?"

"What do you mean?" she asked.

"The way I see it," I said, "looking for love is blocking you from finding love."

"Say that again," she said.

"Looking for love is stopping you from finding love."

"So what do you suggest?"

"Stop looking for love."

Evelyne normally had a fast answer for everything but not this time. She didn't say a word. She went deep inside herself. I waited for her. Waves of emotion began to break across the surface of her face. I could see her frustration, her anger, and, beneath that, a submerged sadness.

"Aren't you tired of looking for love?" I asked.

"Yes, of course," said Evelyne, reaching for a tissue.

"My invitation to you is to stop looking."

"What, and find a proper job?" she retorted, doing her best to inject some humor.

"Just stop," I said.

"But then what?"

This was only our second meeting, but I sensed in Evelyne a readiness to look at things in a new way. So I told Evelyne that the way I saw it, her "looking for love" was an attempt to strike a deal with God. I said, "It's like your ego has given God an ultimatum, which is 'I'll only start to live again once I find love,' or, rather, 'once YOU (God) find me love.' And while this might sound reasonable to your ego, it isn't how God works, and it isn't how life works either. Looking for love isn't how you find love."

"So how do you find love?" asked Evelyne.

"Well, first you have to recognize that you are what you're looking for," I said.

Evelyne didn't say anything, which was her way of saying, "Keep speaking."

"You are still looking for love because you don't feel loveable," I went on. "You've forgotten how loveable you are, and it's this forgetting that's causing you to search for love *and not find it*."

"I don't find me loveable," said Evelyne softly.

"Loveability starts with looking at yourself and finding love there," I told her.

Evelyne was sitting perfectly still in her chair. I could tell that she was testing what I had said against her own logic. A verdict was imminent. In a few moments I would know if we could proceed or not. I could feel her resistance, but I could also see that her face had softened and that she looked younger, brighter, and clearer. Evelyne soon appeared from inside herself, flinging the doors of her mind wide open.

"All right, I'm going to stop looking for love," she said, pausing ever so slightly. "But I still want to find love. So how do I do that?"

"Well, first you have to accept that you are made of love," I explained. "This is important because *like attracts like,* and if you know that you are love, you'll feel comfortable about attracting love into your life."

"Okay, I'll work on that," she said. "But can you give me something more practical to do in the meantime?"

"Yes," I said. "But only if you promise not to overlook what I just said."

"Okay, okay," she replied, widening her eyes at me in an effort to move our conversation along.

"The way to find love is to be a more loving person," I said.

"I am a loving person," she protested.

"I'm asking you to be a *more* loving person," I replied.

"How do I do that?"

"Start by loving everyone more."

"Everyone!" she exclaimed.

"Everyone."

"Are you sure?"

"I'm not asking you to *date* everyone," I said.

"Good."

"Loving everyone is true love," I explained. "It's also the key to being able to love someone."

"So how do I start loving everyone?" Evelyne asked.

"Step one is to offer a little willingness," I said.

"Okay, I can do that. And what is step two?"

"Step two is being open to let LOVE show you how to love everyone. LOVE, which is what you are made of, will show you the way, if you let it."

Looking for love is hell. Everyone's been there. We've all done it. It's a mind-set you identify with when you forget who you are and what love is. It's what you do when you experience the fall from grace and you fear that love has abandoned you. In this hell, you search for love outside of yourself. The searching leads you to believe that you exist outside of love. You act as if you and love are two separate things. You think the purpose of the world is to find love, and then, once you find it, not to lose it again.

Looking for love is frightening. That's because it's a strategy used to conceal a most terrible fear you would rather not look at: the fear that *"I am not loveable."* I refer to this fear as the *basic fear* because we all experience it and also because it gives rise to every other fear. This fear is not real but you don't know that if you're too scared to look at it. So, you decide to leave yourself alone, and you start looking for someone who will find you loveable. This is just as scary, though. Where will you find this person? Are they still available? What if they are gay—or not gay? Do they even exist? Okay, maybe they do exist, but what are the chances of them loving you if you don't love you?

Looking for love is painful. You are looking for love because you have judged yourself to be unloveable. Until you change your mind about yourself, your only hope is to find someone who will overturn this judgment. So you try to create a pleasing image that hides the pain of feeling unloveable. This image knows how to be seductive, to attract attention, and to win admiration, but because it is not the real you, it does not attract real love. Therefore, you keep on looking, but because you won't change your mind about yourself, all you find is your own lovelessness.

It's difficult to believe in love when you are looking for love. The more you keep looking, the more unloveable you feel. Because you don't believe you are loveable, you can't believe it's possible for someone to love you. Eventually, you begin to doubt if love even exists. This is the worst pain of all. To believe that and to keep on living is impossible. Now you are just a shadow of your-self. You have reached a dead end. Looking for love hasn't worked. So now it's time to try something else. And that's a good thing.

**Those that go searching for love
only make manifest their own lovelessness,
and the loveless never find love,
only the loving find love,
and they never have to seek for it.**

D. H. Lawrence[1]

The way out of hell is not to seek for love but to see how you are blocking love. You begin by examining what is causing you to seek for love in the first place. First, you must cast off all the loveless images of yourself that you have made. Looking for love, in its truest sense, isn't about find-ing someone else; it's about find-ing yourself again. You also have to be willing to drop your theories about love, to empty your mind of learned ideas, to let go of old stories, and—as William Blake put it—to "cleanse the doors of per-ception" so as to let love appear as it really is.[2]

> *"To find the beloved, you must become the beloved."*
>
> **Rumi**

Love is an inner journey home. The way to get there is to start here, right where you are now. The goal of this journey is not to find love; it is to know love. This knowledge exists in you already. I call this knowledge *loveability.*

Chapter 1

Love Is Not a Word

"I want to learn how to write," said Bo, my four-year-old daughter, as she burst into my office at the top of our house, waving a crumpled bit of paper and a pink crayon over her head.

"Wonderful," I said.

"I want to learn now," she pleaded.

"Okay, then," I said, turning away from my computer so as to give her my full attention.

"How shall we start?" she asked, crayon at the ready, hovering over the paper, which already had a drawing of a rainbow on it.

"Well, what's the first word you would like to write?"

"Love," said Bo, most emphatically.

"Let's begin," I said.

I guided Bo's hand across the paper as we made an *L* and an *O* and a *V* and an *E*. Once finished, we took a moment to admire our work.

"That's love," I said.

"Really?" asked Bo, who was now on her feet.

"Yes," I said.

"I just wrote my first word!" shouted Bo as she jumped up and down.

"Congratulations!" I shouted back.

Bo carried on being super-excited for a few moments, and then she stopped to look again at the *L*, the *O*, the *V*, and the *E*.

"That's not really love, is it, Daddy?" she asked, looking directly into my eyes.

"Yes, it is," I assured her.

"No, Daddy, it's not."

"Why not?" I asked.

"Love is not a word," she said.

There are 6,909 languages on planet Earth.[1] I imagine that's more than most people would guess. Very few countries have only one language. Papua New Guinea, for instance, has 832 languages. Some languages are more popular than others. Nearly one billion people speak Mandarin. Several languages are spoken by only a handful of people. Recently, the Bo language (not a reference to my daughter!) died out when an 85-year-old member of the Bo tribe in the Indian-owned Andaman islands died.[2] All these languages have a word, a character, or a sound for *love,* and some have many. We all talk about love, and think about love, and yet to understand love we must remember that love is not a word.

As I write this book, my daughter Bo has just turned five years old, and my son Christopher is 16 months old, and they both love to play with words. Bo's vocabulary is growing rapidly. I especially enjoy how she inserts words like *actually* and *splendid* into her speech. Christopher has just begun to speak his first words. *Gar-den* and *spi-der* are popular right now. His favorite word is *boer.* My wife, Hollie, and I have no idea what *boer* means. We aren't even sure if *boer* is the correct spelling. If we had to guess, we'd say that *boer* is Christopher's word for everything that isn't a gar-den or a spi-der.

So what is a word? A word is nothing by itself. It's just a symbol. That's all. It doesn't define *love*; it just tells us that we are speaking of *love.* *Love* is a name for something that is more than just a word. To be on proper speaking terms with love, you must remember this. The problem with talking about "love" with words is that words reduce *love* to an *it,* a *thing* or an object; but real love is not a noun (to find, to have, or to keep). Words also create too much distance between love and you. They make it sound like love is one thing and you are another. No matter which language you speak, something is lost in translation when you rely on words to define love.

"What do you know of Love except the name?" asked Jelaluddin Rumi, the 13th-century Persian poet.[3] Rumi was a gifted wordsmith who wrote as many words on love as anyone who ever lived. Yet even Rumi realized that love couldn't be fully explained with words. In his magnum opus, *Mathnawi*, which contains over 51,000 verses of poetry, Rumi told us:

> Whatever I say to explain or describe Love
> When I arrive at Love itself, I'm ashamed of my words.
> The commentary of words can make things clear—
> But Love without words has more clarity.
> My pen was rushing to write its thoughts down;
> When it came to Love, it broke in two.
> In speaking of Love, the intellect is impotent,
> Like a donkey trapped in a bog:
> Only Love itself can explain Love,
> Only Love can explain the destiny of lovers.
> The proof of the sun is the sun itself:
> If you want proof, don't turn your face away.[4]

To know love, you must first accept that love cannot be defined. No amount of words can define love, because love is not just a name. The intellect can't define love, because the intellect deals with ideas, and love is not just an idea. No one person holds the copyright on love, because love is bigger than all humanity. Religion cannot define love, because love is too spiritual for any one religion. Science cannot define love either, because the essence of love cannot be trapped in test tubes and split apart in particle accelerators.

But keep faith! Just because love cannot be defined, it doesn't mean that you can't get to know love. It's worth remembering that many of the most interesting things in life cannot be defined. Their indefinable quality is part of their wonder and majesty. Psychologists aren't able to define the psyche, and yet we keep on exploring the mind. Priests who worship God accept that, in truth, there is no name for God. Physicists now recognize that the universe is made up of energy, but they can't define what energy is. "It is important to realize that in physics today, we have no knowledge what energy is," said Richard Feynman, winner of the Nobel Prize for Physics.[5]

Some people have said that love cannot be defined because love is coy, and mysterious, and elusive, and it likes to play tricks with us. From these descriptions it is clear to me that love has been endowed with the qualities of a man or woman who is rejecting sexual and romantic advances. This is another case of projection closing the doors of perception. My personal experience is that love can be known, just not defined. Love is available to everyone, without exception. Love has already been given to us; now all we have to do is give ourselves to love.

> *"Love wishes to be known, completely understood and shared. It has no secrets, nothing that it would keep apart and hide."*
>
> *A Course in Miracles*

I like to think of the word *love* as a door. If you only look at the door, all you get is an idea about what love is; but if you are willing to move closer to the door, to open it, and to walk on through, you get to have an experience of what love is. To be intimate with love, you have to move beyond words, leave behind self-concepts, empty your mind of learned ideas, stop being so religious, and let yourself dissolve into love. Now we are really getting somewhere. Now, at last, we can stop trying to define love, and we can let love define us.

When I began my inquiry into love, I thought I had to define it before I could think about it! But my attempts to define love came to nothing. No arrangement of words or ideas could capture the whole truth. When I couldn't define love, I was tempted to stop my inquiry. *There's no point studying something you can't define,* I thought. Despite my frustration, I stuck with my inquiry because I understood somehow that, even though love can't be defined, the heart knows what love is. *Love cannot be defined, but it can be recognized.* And so I'd say to myself, "I want to know about love," and then I'd pay attention. And keep on paying attention. That's all that any of us have to do. And when we do this, we make a joyful discovery, which is that *love will teach us what love is.*

"Let your teacher be Love itself."

Rumi[6]

Chapter 2

Your Eternal Loveliness

Why are babies so loveable? And what does this teach us about love and our own true nature?

Babies hold our attention like nothing else. We gaze into their eyes, we watch their every move, we snap countless photos, and we study them while they sleep. When I first met my daughter, Bo, I held her in my arms, and we peered into each other's eyes for what felt like forever. When I welcomed my son, Christopher, into the world, I was transfixed by his presence, and I couldn't take my eyes off him. I've always found babies, not just my own, to be wondrous and fascinating, and I know I'm not alone in this. So what is it we are seeing when we look at a baby?

Babies are generally short, chubby, and toothless, without much hair, and they leak a lot at both ends. Every baby looks perfect, even ones with missing stomachs, chromosomal abnormalities, and crippled limbs. Is this because their nostrils are often heart-shaped? When you really pay attention to babies, you notice that their bodies are still in soft focus. They are barely physical. The soul dances lightly across the body. They are pure energy. They are a vibration of love. They are *a lively flame* that is not weary, or tired, or confounded.[1]

When you pay attention to a baby, you notice how naked he or she is. Babies haven't put anything on themselves yet. They have no masks, no personas, no armor, and no dark glasses. They are still wearing what Zen Buddhists call the *Original Face.*[2] They aren't putting on a face for the world to see. What you are witnessing is their true nature. They aren't trying to be someone, to be nice, to look good, or to be interesting. There are no pretenses. There is no deceit. There is no attempt to create a pleasing image. They aren't trying to be loveable; they just are.

Babies are still close to the *Unconditioned Self,* which is the name I give for our true self. They haven't yet learned to identify with gender. They don't know if they are American or Chinese. They don't care if they are black or white. They aren't interested in what religion their parents follow. They haven't had time yet to make up a story to tell about how elusive love is, or how difficult love is, or how worthy or unworthy they are of love. They don't judge themselves. They carry no grievances. They are not cynical yet. Have you ever met a cynical baby?

Babies embody the *basic truth* about us, which is that we are all loveable. When you look at a baby, you can see what St. Francis of Assisi called our *eternal loveliness.* You see this eternal loveliness because you are looking with your heart, not just your physical eyes. At the same time, babies mirror your own eternal loveliness back to you. They show you *your* original face. Their eternal loveliness is a reflection of your Unconditioned Self. St. Francis of Assisi taught us that everyone is an expression of God's eternal loveliness. Moreover, he recognized that every animal, every plant, and every form of life is an expression of love.

God extended himself in love, and we are all expressions of this love. This is the Original Blessing we share with each other.[3] There are no exceptions to this. None. The basic truth about you is "I am loveable." Everybody's basic truth is "I am loveable." This is true whether you remember or forget it. It is also true whether you believe it or not. Our Unconditioned Self is a consciousness of love that extends from the heart of God into the body of all creation.

The word *love* and the word *God* are both pointing toward the same thing. They are both pointing at each of us.

The Original Blessing cannot be undone. Your eternal loveliness has no end. "You were created to be completely loved and completely loveable for your whole life," says Deepak Chopra in *The Path to Love*.[4] This is all true. However, as the baby grows and takes on the conditioning of this world, it is possible to forget about love. A *learned self* takes the place of the Unconditioned Self. This learned self is just a shadow; it is not real. However, when you identify with this learned self, you forget the basic truth "I am loveable." In this forgetting, the basic fear "I am not loveable" takes hold. And so, as Galway Kinnell wrote in his poem *Saint Francis and the Sow,* "sometimes it is necessary to reteach a thing its loveliness."[5]

> *"Love is our highest word and the synonym for God."*
>
> **Ralph Waldo Emerson**

You are made of love, and this is the key to knowing how to love and be loved. Your purpose is to be an instrument of this love. It is to extend this love through all your relationships with parents, siblings, friends, lovers, children, strangers, enemies, and the world over. How do you do this? You start by identifying with love. Love is your original energy. It is the heart of who you are. It is the natural expression of your Unconditioned Self and your *eternal loveliness*. When you remember this, you realize that, in truth, you already know how to love and be loved.

Identify with love, and you are safe.
Identify with love, and you are home.
Identify with love, and find your Self.

A Course in Miracles[6]

Chapter 3

Our Shared Purpose

Growing up, I learned to believe that my destiny was to find one special person to love so that we could both live happily ever after. I lived in a little village in the south of England. It was very little. It was called Littleton. Hardly anyone lived there. I didn't like any of the girls in Littleton enough to fall in love with. There was one girl, called Claire, but she didn't like me. She liked every other boy but not me. Beverley, who was in my class, told everyone I was her boyfriend, but we never even kissed. The girl I really liked was Marie Osmond, the one who sang "Paper Roses." It didn't work out with Marie, though, largely because we never met.

At school, there never was a class about love. Our curriculum was full of supposedly more important things like algebra and economics. My teenage years were full of longing for love and angst about love. Thinking about love made me feel happy, lonely, and desperate. I loved school dances. We all danced like crazy to Michael Jackson, Stevie Wonder, and the Bee Gees. It was so much fun learning the new moves and making each other laugh. At the end of the evening the slow songs started, usually with "I Want to Know What Love Is" by Foreigner. Suddenly we were serious and neurotic. Who should I dance with? Where should I put my hands? Where are they putting their hands? Are we going to kiss? Do we have to kiss?

My first conscious inquiry into love had nothing to do with girls, though. When I was 15 years old, my mum, my brother, and I learned that my dad was drinking heavily. Though Dad promised to stop drinking many times, he and my mum eventually separated. "I love your father, but we can't live together," she told us. We all loved my dad. And Dad loved my mum. And Dad loved (adored and worshipped, more like) his sons. But Dad was not well. He wouldn't let himself be helped. Our family was broken. Dad continued to drink. Over the next ten years, he lived homeless for long periods of time, dying gradually, in slow motion, due to some kind of lovelessness.

My dad's drinking and my mother's depression, which is another story, catapulted me into an inquiry that I didn't feel ready for. I danced clumsily with the big questions like "What is life for?" and "What is real?" I was just a kid. How was I meant to answer these questions? My teachers at school weren't any help. One day, our head teacher announced that we were going to have a career-counseling class. He said it had something to do with the rest of our life. A teacher we hadn't met before led the class. She introduced herself to us and told us that it was important for us to start thinking about a career.

"What's your name?" she asked, pointing at me.

"Robert Holden," I said.

"What sort of a career do you want, Robert?"

I had no idea what to say. I hadn't thought about it. She kept looking at me. I couldn't find any words to say. She kept on looking at me. I prayed that she'd move on to someone else, but she didn't.

"Robert, what sort of a career do you want?" she asked again.

"Oh, that's very kind," I said finally, "but I don't want one, thanks."

"You have to have a career, Robert," she said.

"Really?" I asked.

"Yes," she assured me.

"Please don't worry about me," I said. "Honestly, I'll be fine."

I had too much going on in my life to think about a career. My dad had a career, and look what happened to him. The teacher left me alone while she interrogated the rest of my friends. "Who here wants to be a teacher?" she asked. No one raised a hand. None of us wanted to be teachers. That would mean coming back to school. "Who here wants to work in a bank?" she asked. My friend sitting next to me raised his hand. I was shocked. We'd never talked about banking before. I found out later that his father worked in a bank. "Who here wants to work with their hands?" she asked. One by one, all my friends raised their hands for something or other. Clearly, this wasn't just a conversation we were having; this was decision time.

"So, Robert Holden, you've had some time to think," she said when everyone else had answered.

"Yes, it's been very thought provoking," I said.

"Well?"

"Well what?"

"Your career," she said.

"My career," I said.

"Robert, we haven't got all day."

This was a truly surreal moment. I was the last item on her list. If she could get me, she had done her job. I'd had more than 50 minutes to work out what I wanted to do with the rest of my life. I wanted to help her out. I really did.

"Robert, you have to choose something," she said.

"I know."

"So, what do you choose?"

"It's a close call," I said, stalling for a bit more time.

"Say something, Robert," she urged me.

"Philosophy," I shouted out.

My friends started laughing, which wasn't the response I had expected. She wasn't laughing, however.

"Philosophy!" she said, like the words came out of her nose.

"Yes, philosophy," I repeated, and I noticed I liked the sound of what I had just said.

"What sort of philosophy?" she asked.

"Greek!" I said, this time playing for a laugh, which I got from my friends, but not from her.

Anyone can be a philosopher, I suppose. You don't need any formal qualifications. No one can tell you that you're not a philosopher. To be a philosopher, all you need is a sense of wonder, some curiosity, and an open mind. You also must like asking questions. I was certainly asking a lot of questions at that time in my life. Most children do. Young children in particular ask questions all day long 'and out loud. The other day, my daughter, Bo, asked me, "Why does love feel so nice, Daddy?" In the same conversation, she asked me, "Why do we have skin?" and also "Does wind come from the sneeze of a cloud?" As children get older, they still have questions, just like I did, but they carry the questions more privately. Hopefully, we never stop asking questions.

My mum would tell you that I was a thoughtful child. I kept my bedroom tidy and took off my shoes at the door, but that's not the sort of thoughtfulness I mean. As a child, I was full of thinking. My sense of wonder stayed with me. I wanted to know about life. Real life. Not just what happened in 1066 and at the Battle of Hastings. Real life. This curiosity was heightened by my dad's drinking, my mother's depression, and that ridiculous career-counseling class. I thought a lot about happiness, and success, and God, and careers, and girls, and everything else. Everything I thought about pointed me back to one thing, which was love.

The more I thought about love, the more I had to admit to myself how important love was. I could see that the urge to love and be loved is our primary desire. Love is as important to us as air, water, and food. A life without love isn't a life. The more you love and also let yourself be loved, the more alive you feel. This primary desire is something we share with each other: we all want to experience love, to know we are loveable, and to be loving people. Love feeds all our basic desires, including our desire to be connected, to be known, to be safe, to be happy, to

> *"Love is the life of man."*
>
> **Emanuel Swedenborg**

be successful, and to be free. Love is the stuff of life. Even I could see that, and I was only 16 years old.

I understood that love was important, but what I couldn't understand was why people didn't talk more about love. The Beatles were singing about love. So too were Stevie Wonder, and Bob Dylan, and Van Morrison, and Joni Mitchell. There's no such thing as too many love songs. At the same time, our favorite authors and poets send more love stories and love notes into the world. Love is all around us, but we don't talk about love that much. Politicians don't. Newscasters don't. Schoolteachers don't. My friends didn't. We talked about girls but not love. Conversations about love—real love—are thin on the ground, especially when you consider that every day we buy a million love songs and read a million love stories.

My mum and dad always told my brother and me how much they loved us. But we didn't talk about love. My first conversation about love with my mum happened soon after my dad left home. We talked about Dad, how much we loved him, and how we wished he could love himself. We talked about Mum's depression and what it was like for her when she felt unloveable. We talked about her childhood and also Dad's childhood. She told me stories about Dad and his service in the navy in World War II. I didn't even know my dad had fought in the war. She told me stories about battleships, torpedoes, a sea on fire, his friends' mortal wounds, and the other acts of war he witnessed. Dad loved us, but he also had a history that didn't love him.

The more I paid attention to love, the more I realized how necessary love is. Love is an essential growth ingredient in your life. From conception, love is helping to birth you into the world. The study of evolutionary psychology recognizes that love is a basic growth medium of cells. Love matters, because when children are loved it influences the central dogma of their DNA, develops their nervous systems, and helps to build their brains.[1] Love helps us to grow, and not just in the early stages of our life, but in every stage thereafter. Scientists tell us that this is true not just for humans but for other animals too.[2]

When you remember the basic truth "I am loveable," this helps you to evolve in the direction of love. When you choose love, you prosper. Conversely, when you believe the basic fear "I am not loveable," you stop growing in the direction of love. My dad had forgotten about his eternal loveliness. He was trying to love us, but he didn't love himself or his history. His drinking was his way of trying to drown the basic fear.

When your dad lives homeless, you're never sure when you'll meet up next or where. He always kept in touch, though, and we usually met up once a fortnight or so. We talked about a lot of things, including love. "All that matters is love," I told him. And he said, "All that matters to me is that you know I love you."

> *"In love lies the seed of our growth."*
>
> **Paulo Coelho**

My view of love was expanding. Love wasn't just about girlfriends, romance, and sex anymore. Love wasn't just an emotion. Love wasn't just about family or the people you like. I began to see that love is about everything—that it's about our whole life. When you make love your purpose, you are fulfilling your destiny. You didn't come here to make yourself into somebody; you came here to be what you already are, which is the presence of love. That's what's meant to happen, but then we take the detour into fear and get distracted and lost. Now we have to turn to love again, so as to be saved and so that we can keep on loving and being loved.

Life is all about love, and even when it isn't, it still is, really. Love is what you are busy with, even when it may look like you are busy with something else. We all get busy, chasing our careers, paying the mortgage, doing the school run. It's hard not to get distracted in the daily blur of our lives. Life can be a full-time preoccupation. But when we come to our senses, which we inevitably do, we know that love is our purpose, love is our delight, and love is our salvation. Nothing else matters quite so much. Love comes first; everything else is secondary.

Thinking about love, and talking about love, helped me to get clearer about some of the other big questions in life. What I came to see back then, and know for sure now, is that the simple mathematics of love is: the more you love, the more you grow; the more you love, the healthier you are; the more you love, the happier you feel; the more you love, the more successful you are. Conversely, not loving enough and feeling unloved are the root causes of every problem and conflict in your life and on our planet. In sum, *your life works when you love, and it doesn't when you don't.*

The real work of your life is to know how to love and be loved. This is our shared purpose. It is the purpose of your life and the purpose of humanity. Despite what you have been taught, the purpose of existence is not solely to grow more dollars, more yen, and more Euros. Your real employment is not to acquire job titles, conquer the market, and kill the opposition. The goal of your life is not to inflate yourself into an ego that is bigger, smarter, or more powerful than another ego. None of this is real. These are all trivial pursuits. How would it really profit you if you gained the whole world and you forgot about love along the way?

Chapter 4

Ground of Love

There were no lectures on love when I studied psychology. Things are changing now, but love is still the road less traveled in universities and colleges in the Western world.[1] My classes were interesting but not enlightening. We studied a self with no soul and a mind with no heart, and the body of our work was full of disease and anxiety. There was no joy. Love was absent. A lecture on something called Interpersonal Attraction Theory flirted with love, but only a little. No one addressed love directly, not even Carl Jung, who wrote about everything. It was as if we had forgotten that love existed, or maybe we were avoiding it.

Mostly we studied Sigmund Freud. Freud stated that "the communal life of human beings" (his own term) had a twofold foundation, which was love and work.[2] "Love and work is all there is," he wrote. Reading what Freud had to say about love was hard work, certainly. Here again, I found that love was not addressed directly. Even his book *Psychology of Love* is mostly taken up with commentary about ego and libido, Narcissus and Oedipus, and eroticism and neurosis. "One is very crazy when in love," wrote Freud, echoing the thoughts of Plato and Friedrich Nietzsche and others.[3] However, Freud also wrote this about love:

> A strong egoism is a protection against disease, but in
> the last resort we must begin to love in order that we may

not fall ill, and must fall ill if, in consequence of frustration, we cannot love.[4]

Freud taught that separation is the root cause of suffering. All our fears, our unworthiness, our aloneness—the entire A to Z of misery—is caused by our sense of anxious apartness. This separation happens in the mind. It's like a lucid dream. In the dream, we make a separate ego-self. I refer to this self in my work as the learned self, which is what we identify with when we forget about the Unconditioned Self. This ego-self is governed by a superego, which is a self-made god that reigns high in clouds of conscience. The ego-self is not sure what it is. Feelings of anxious apartness give rise to questions like "Am I real?" and "Is there a God?" and "Does love even exist?" What the ego-self really wants to know is "Am I loveable?"

Freud taught that the anxious apartness causes you to feel split off from your true self and alienated from others.[5] A loss of intimacy with yourself makes empathy with others impossible. Genuine contact with others is lost in a world full of egos, personas, and masks. Freud used the word *object* a lot in his work.[6] One of the terrifying effects of separation is that the ego-self, which is the central object of our dreams, turns everything else into separate objects too, including mothers, fathers, lovers, God, and also love. Even your heart is turned into an object, like a small stone, which you can think about, but not feel.

This was the first time I had read about the theory of separation and anxious apartness. *Revelation* is a big word, and I am reluctant to use it, but I must, because this was revelatory for me. Freud was showing me that *all my pain* was caused by this one basic problem, the problem of separation. Not just my pain, but also my dad's pain, my mum's pain, and everyone else's pain is caused by this anxious apartness. Freud helped me to take the first step in undoing the hypnosis of separation. In the future, I would read more about the illusion of separation and its dreadful effects in spiritual literature, in medical journals, in books on physics, and elsewhere, and I would also learn more about how to undo the illusion.

Freud gave me a lot to think about. He shone a light into the dark places of the mind where we hide so many blocks to love. I am in awe of his courage and determination to keep on exposing the blocks to love's awareness. It clearly took a huge personal toll on him to do so. Freud gave us a psychology of the ego, and in doing so he showed us how we make it so difficult to love and be loved. However, there was something missing in Freud's work and that was love itself.

Freud's psychology didn't have much *psyche*, or soul, in it. He didn't study love directly. His view of love was limited and distorted by his focus on sex. Could it really be true that the love I felt for my parents was just a cover for my wish to sexually possess my mother and to kill my father? My story was that I fancied Marie Osmond not my mum. I imagine Freud would have interpreted my story as a classic case of repression or displacement. Sex can be an expression of love (or not), but love is more than just sex. Freud carried the torch so far, so that it could be passed on to people like Alfred Adler, Viktor Frankl, Erich Fromm, and others.

What I understand now—and what I teach in *Loveability*—is that love can wake you up from the hypnosis of separation. Love offers you the total release of all your mistaken ideas about yourself. It empties your mind of every victim, villain, and hero that was lost in a dream. It frees you from the anxious apartness that is the ego-consciousness. Love brings you back to the Unconditioned Self. Love helps you take your place again in the heart of creation. In truth, you'd never left. It was all just a dream. The ego was asleep, but your heart (the essence of who you are) was awake and watching over you. Love reveals that you exist in love, always.

Love is a joyful dance that cultivates intimacy with yourself and empathy with another. As you connect consciously with your Unconditioned Self, every persona, mask, and self-concept falls away and you experience intimacy with your true nature. This intimacy in you extends itself and is translated into empathy with your family, your friends, your lover, your children, your colleagues, and everyone else. Intimacy and empathy are non-ego states. They are expressions of our oneness. They are the basis for real openness, honest communication, and true friendship. They also reveal that we exist in what Thomas Merton, the Catholic monk, called "that hidden ground of Love for which there can be no explanations."[7]

Love arises when you realize we are all part of the same creation, a shared consciousness, and a universal heart. You and I exist together in love. Just because you may read a different Bible than I read does not mean we can tear up the oneness of the universe. We exist in each other. The Unconditioned Self that I think is mine is also yours. The ego that you think is yours doesn't belong to anyone, not even you. There is no separation in love. We are made of the same love *and* we are free to express this love in our own unique way. This is how love dances with itself.

> *"One love,*
> *one heart,*
> *one destiny."*
>
> **Often attributed**
> **to Bob Marley**

Love is the hidden ground upon which we are all dancing. This love is the essence and expression of what oneness is. This love can only be appreciated when we stop trying to divide it up into different designations, different types, and different levels. All love comes from one heart. Love has many expressions, but it is always the same love. What makes love so powerful and beautiful is that it includes us all, wholly, and without any exception. In *A Course in Miracles* there is a passage that sums this up very well:

> Perhaps you think that different kinds of love are possible. Perhaps you think there is a kind of love for this, a kind for that; a way of loving one, another way of loving still another. Love is one. It has no separate parts and no degrees; no kinds nor levels, no divergences and no distinctions. It is like itself, unchanged throughout. It never alters with a person or a circumstance. It is the Heart of God, and also of His Son.[8]

My inquiry into separation showed me that, when you look into separation, it's impossible to find it. It's not really there. It really is just a trick of perception. I also discovered that in the mind of love there are no pronouns. What "I" do to "you" is no different from what "I" do to "me." Because of our oneness, "I" experience the effects of everything "I" do to "you." That's why kindness is a blessing that blesses us to the power of three: "me," "you," and "all of us." Conversely, that's why violence is not smart. Like the sting of a bee, the poison is released inside and out. Attacking another is a form of self-harm. You can't attack someone and know who you really are.

Love is also grounded in an attitude of compassion. Compassion is necessary for our survival and our evolution. Compassion is an attitude that upholds the memory of wholeness for people when they are lost in separation, pain, and conflict. Compassion is love's holding environment. It is how love whispers to us, "I will remember the truth of who you are even when you cannot remember this for yourself." This compassion sees through what Einstein called the "optical delusion" of separation. Einstein taught us that we can free ourselves from identifying with this ego-consciousness by "widening our circle of compassion to embrace all living creatures and the whole of nature and its beauty."[9]

To love and be loved is the true joy of every human heart. There is no higher happiness than this. Alas, in any human drama there are also wounds and disappointments, mistakes and betrayals, pain and heartache. Even so, love comes to our rescue. Love offers us a solution, which is a process called *forgiveness*. Forgiveness is an angel that comes to us when we sleep and wakes us from the hypnosis. It is the ground of love that supports you when you are falling, breaking apart, and coming undone. Forgiveness undoes the blocks to love's awareness. It shows you that a universe of love doesn't ever stop, even when all you can see is pain. Love always loves you, even when you can't or won't love yourself.

Chapter 5

Live Your Love

I met my first spiritual teacher when I was taking a course called Communications at university in Birmingham.[1] His name was Avanti Kumar, and he was in the same course as me. He was different from the rest of us. We were all regular students and he was what the lecturers called "a mature student." We were 18 years old, and he was 24. That made him very mature in our eyes. Ancient, even. Avanti always sat at the back of the class. He was always the last to arrive and the first to leave. We knew nothing about him, but there was definitely something about him, and that made him the most interesting person in the class.

My first conversation with Avanti happened about six weeks into the first term. It went a bit like this:

"Hi, my name is Robert," I said.

"Yes, I know," said Avanti.

"So, how are you enjoying the class?" I asked.

"Quite so," he replied.

"What made you choose this class?"

"I came to meet you," he said.

"Great," I said.

"Yes," he said.

"Thanks," I said.

And that was that. But after that, we began a series of conversations that would change the course of my life. Avanti was a student of yoga. Not the sort of yoga that is full of forward bends and salutations to the sun. His yoga was a spiritual philosophy called Advaita Vedanta. *Advaita* means "nonduality." The first precept of this path is that oneness is our reality and separation is an illusion. Avanti was conversant with many schools of philosophy, metaphysics, and religion, so talking with him was always thrilling. He was the first person in my life with whom I could properly explore the big questions—the questions like "Who am I?" and "What is real?" and, of course, "What is love?"

The first book Avanti gave me to read was *The Bhagavad Gita.* The version he gave me was the translation by Juan Mascaró, whose introduction is every bit as compelling as the main text.[2] Thirty years later, I still have the copy Avanti gave me, and it is very well thumbed. The *Gita,* for short, is a poem about Creation and the nature of reality. For the first time in my life I was reading direct references to love. I was learning that love is not just an emotion, or a feeling, or some pleasant chemistry in the brain, but that love is intelligent, and wise, and the essential energy of creation. Albert Einstein is often quoted as having said, "When I read the Bhagavad-Gita and reflect about how God created this universe everything else seems so superfluous." The *Gita* blew my mind, too.

Avanti also introduced me to Bhakti Yoga, which is a spiritual philosophy based entirely on love. According to Bhakti Yoga, which I first read about in the *Gita,* love is recognized as a spiritual path that leads to self-realization and real happiness. Love is the mind of God. Love is what you experience when you join your mind with the mind of God. Love is how you think with God. Therefore, and this is a very big therefore, *love is your real mind.* When you really let yourself feel love and you let all other thoughts drop away, you have contacted the consciousness that is the mind of your Unconditioned Self.

Avanti gave me many more books to read, including *Autobiography of a Yogi* by Paramahansa Yogananda. This memoir tells the story of Paramahansa's childhood in Uttar Pradesh, his encounters with saints and gurus across India, and also his journey to America, where he taught meditation and yoga until his death in 1952. Paramahansa's beautiful storytelling touched me deeply. He taught that the purpose of life is to experience a divine romance with God and with each other. The only reason for being on "this little patch of the Milky Way," as he put it, is to understand the holy science of love.[3]

"Love is the door," said Paramahansa Yogananda, "both to the mind of God and to the heart of who you are."[4] He taught his students to meditate on love so as to realize the oneness that exists between God, self, and one another. His encouragement to everyone was to make love a daily practice and to live your love. To many people, Paramahansa Yogananda was the embodiment of Bhakti Yoga, the spiritual path of love. He described love as our greatest joy—the key to our happiness—and also as the spiritual solution to every psychological and social problem in this world.

Avanti had set me on my path with a heart.[5] My studies took me to many places, including India, where I visited Bodhgaya and sat under the Bodhi Tree where it is said that the Buddha received his enlightenment. By now I wasn't just reading about love; I was also meditating on love. The more I tuned in directly to love, the more I could see that love is the light of our mind. It is a pristine state of consciousness that has zero mass. In other words, love is what you experience when you empty your mind of attachments to judgment, self-criticism, unworthiness, resentment, cynicism, and fear.

> *"Instead of trying to stop thought when you meditate, focus your attention on love."*
>
> **Ramana Maharshi**

While I was in Bodhgaya, I made friends with a Burmese Buddhist monk. "Let me tell you a little secret about my friend the Buddha," he said. "The Buddha is not my real teacher, you know. My real teacher is the loving kindness that is in my mind. This is what my friend the Buddha revealed to me." I was so struck by what this monk had said to me that I asked him to say it again so I could write it down in my journal. And now, 20 years later, I get to share it with you. The Buddhist monk also shared this story with me:

> The Buddha was sitting by a campfire beneath a canvas full of stars one night. Some friends joined him. They began to ask the Buddha questions like "What is life for?" and "What is the Self made of?" and "Is there a God?" and "How do we get to heaven?" The Buddha waited until every question was spoken. Then he answered, "If you practice loving kindness you will know the answer to every question there is. Enlightenment does not bring love; love is what brings enlightenment."

One week after my first trip to India, I visited a mind/body/ spirit festival at the Royal Horticultural Halls in London. I was exploring one of the many esoteric bookstalls there when I came across a big green book, some 1,400 pages long, called *A Course in Miracles.* I bought the book mainly because I liked the title. At the time, I had no idea that I had found what is, to me, the most beautiful book on love ever written. *A Course in Miracles* stayed on one of my bookshelves for a year or so before I got around to reading it. Even when I did pick it up, I put it down a few times, unable to get into it. Something in me made me persevere, and I am glad it did.

A Course in Miracles is a course on love. "This is a course on love, because it is about you," it states in the text.[6] *A Course in Miracles* is written in Christian language, and it is full of iambic pentameter, which is the meter that Shakespeare often used. I found that the poetry of this book had the effect of disengaging my intellect. Often, by the time I had reached the bottom of the page, I had completely forgotten what I had just read. Initially, I found it difficult to understand *A Course in Miracles,* and yet on every page there were gems like:

**You are the work of God,
and His work is wholly loveable**

and wholly loving.
This is how a man must
think of himself in his heart,
because this is what he is.[7]

A Course in Miracles teaches that you have two selves, one real and one imagined. The real self is called the God-Self, or Christ, which is the one that God made. This Self is what I call your Unconditioned Self. It is your eternal loveliness. The imagined self is called the ego, which is self-made. *A Course in Miracles* explains that the mind of the God-Self is love and that the mind of separated ego is fear. "You have but two emotions [love and fear]," it states. "And one you made and one was given you. Each is a way of seeing, and different worlds arise from their different sights."[8] The goal of *A Course in Miracles* is to return us to the awareness of our real mind by choosing love over fear.

A Course in Miracles includes a workbook that has a spiritual lesson for each day of the year. These lessons have been part of my daily spiritual practice for the last 18 years. I think of *A Course in Miracles* as a love letter written by the soul to the ego. When I meditate on my daily lesson, I feel as if I am taking personal tuition from the mind of unconditional love. *A Course in Miracles* teaches that love is our true power and that when we place our faith in love it blesses our life and all of our relationships. It says:

> Put all your faith in the love of God within you; eternal, changeless and forever unfailing. This is the answer to whatever confronts you today. Through the Love of God within you, you can resolve all seeming difficulties without effort and in sure confidence. Tell yourself this often today. It is a declaration of release from the belief in idols. It is your acknowledgement of the truth about yourself.[9]

The day after I completed a calendar year of daily lessons from *A Course in Miracles,* I received a cassette tape with a recording of a talk given by Tom Carpenter.[10] Tom is a teacher of *A*

Course in Miracles and the founder of The Forgiveness Network. His talk was about love, self-acceptance, and forgiveness. It was beautiful. I learned that Tom lived on Kauai, in Hawaii. I also learned that he was about to travel to New York to give a workshop. Quite uncharacteristically of me, I phoned Tom and invited him to extend his trip and visit England to give some talks and to stay at my home. He thanked me for my offer and told me he would think it over. I took that to mean "No." At least I had tried. A day or two later, Tom called to say that he and his wife, Linda, would love to visit.

Tom Carpenter has been my friend and mentor ever since we first met. We have lived in each other's homes for several weeks at a time. We have enjoyed countless dialogues on love. We have taught public courses together. We have dedicated books we have written to each other. We have made a DVD on *A Dialogue on Forgiveness*.[11] Tom taught me, by his loving presence, that love is always present in our mind and that love will show you how to love. I learned from Tom that love is not just a technique you learn, a skill you acquire, or a secret you find on the last page of a book; it is a natural ability that flows effortlessly through you when you let it.

Tom often uses the phrase "Presence of Love" when he speaks and writes. I use it too, because of Tom. It's a beautiful phrase that reminds us that love is always present. In truth, you don't have to invoke love, as the old priests taught us. To invoke suggests that love has to come from somewhere else, but, in truth, love is already present. All you need to do is tune in to love. Love is here, because you are here. Love is a guide that guides you from within yourself. Love helps you to listen to the intelligence of your heart, to think the thoughts of God, and to be more present in your life.

> *"We can only learn to love by loving."*
>
> **Iris Murdoch**

Loveability, which is about knowing how to love and be loved, begins with a conscious decision to be a truly loving presence in your life and everyone else's life, too. Another way of saying this is: *to know what love is, you have to be willing to live your love.* Setting an intention to be a loving presence in this world is the first real step on love's path. Now you are a student of love. Now love has permission to guide you. Now you are in touch with something bigger than your ego, wiser than your intellect, and powerful beyond measure. As Tom once said to me:

**The decision to be the presence of
love is the most powerful influence
you can have in any situation
in your life and in this world.**

PART II

Love Is Who You Are

My friend Adam Green got all the girls at school. It didn't make sense. Adam had acne. His was the worst acne in our class. Adam's hair was black and greasy. He wore thick-rimmed glasses. He carried a lot of weight. He wasn't just big or fat; he was round. I'd say he was at least 15 kilos heavier than me. He perspired a lot, and sometimes his sweat was smelly. Adam wore red shoes, a lime-green sweater, and black jeans. He didn't care what he wore. But Adam got all the girls. Even the pretty ones. It wasn't fair.

Adam was half-Italian. His mother was very Italian. She was a dinner lady at our school. His father was English. He was a bus driver. I remember one time, Adam's mum marched up to him in the playground and started shouting in her strong Italian accent, "Adam! Why you tell people your dad has only one leg? It's not true. He still has two legs. Not just one." Another time, at Adam's home, Mrs. Green called Adam and me into the kitchen. She had just gotten off the phone. "Adam, why you tell people your dad ran you over with his bus?" she yelled. Then she looked at me and cried, "Robert, why is Adam like this? Why is he not a normal boy?"

Adam read *The Financial Times,* and he was only 14 years old. He liked punk music. We played in a band called Nervous. I didn't like punk music, but I liked the guitar, and I liked hanging out with Adam. Adam went on marches for nuclear disarmament. He wrote a song for Nervous called "Whatcha Gonna Do if There's a Nuclear War?" Adam was a member of Greenpeace, and he often reprimanded his mum for not doing enough to save the environment. "What is he saying, Robert?" she would ask. Adam was definitely not normal, nor was he trying to be. He wasn't into looking good. He didn't care about his image. He wasn't trying to be somebody. He wasn't trying to be cool. He was free of all that.

One time, when I was 15 years old, I contracted impetigo on my face. Impetigo is a contagious bacterial infection that causes sores and blisters on the skin. I ended up with a big sore on my right cheek that looked like one of those dark dried apricots. I was afraid I'd be scarred for life. I never expected to get a scar. Why did I have to get impetigo on my face, of all places? How was I ever going to get a girlfriend now? I didn't like what I saw in the mirror. Most of my friends avoided me like the plague. Adam Green didn't. "I like your impetigo," he said. "It makes your face look interesting." Adam assured me that it would be the making of me if I ended up with a scar.

Word got out that Adam Green was dating Kate Tucker. Kate was gorgeous. I couldn't believe it. Yet again, Adam was dating another potential girlfriend of mine. When I next saw him, I asked him, "Is it true you're going out with Kate?"

"Yeah," said Adam casually, as if nothing wonderful and amazing and super was happening in his life.

"Kate Tucker?" I asked, double-checking the facts.

"Yes, Kate Tucker."

"Adam, how do you do it?"

"Do what?"

"How is it that you get all the girls, and I don't?"

"Don't you know?"

"No," I said.

Our conversation was full of fun, but it turned serious when Adam said something that landed like a whack on my head. Here's how the conversation went:

"I'll tell you why I get the girls and you don't," said Adam.

"Great," I said.

"It's easy."

"Tell me, then."

"I love myself."

"Is that it?" I asked.

"Yeah," he said. "And you don't love yourself, Robert. Not yet, anyway."

This was the first time I'd heard someone say out loud, "I love myself." I was stunned. Saying "I love myself" wasn't supposed to be a good thing; it was wrong, illegal, bad, and blasphemous. At school, the worst insult you could throw at anyone was, "You must really love yourself." Self-love was, we assumed, full of conceit and false pride; and yet Adam wasn't ashamed to say it. It was clear to me that when Adam said, "I love myself," he wasn't meaning to say, "I'm more loveable than you, Robert." Adam simply loved himself. He was comfortable in his own skin. He enjoyed being Adam Green. Could this be why all the girls enjoyed being with him?

Adam had pointed out that I didn't love myself. He wasn't being unkind. He was making an observation. And he was right. I could never have said, "I love myself" and felt okay about it. My lack of self-love was my guilty secret. I tried to cover it up by being popular, being the best at sports, and playing guitar in a band. I worked hard to manage people's perceptions of me. I tried to be a "good son" for my parents, a "polite child" for my teachers, and a "loyal friend" to my friends. I would flinch at the slightest hint of disapproval or rejection. I had no idea why I felt like this. I hadn't done anything wrong. I wasn't a bad person. I just didn't feel loveable.

Back then, if someone had asked me a question like "What do you love about yourself?"—which is what I ask people in my Love-ability program—I wouldn't have had an answer to give. What is self-love anyway? I envied my friends who appeared more confident than I felt. I was shocked when the prettiest girl in my class tried to kill herself with a drug overdose after her boyfriend finished with her. I wanted to like myself more, but I didn't know how to do that by myself. Who was this "self" that I was trying to love? How can you love yourself—or even like yourself—if you don't know who you are? I was too busy trying on faces to know myself yet.

My young teenage self had forgotten about the Unconditioned Self. He had lost sight of his eternal loveliness, the original blessing, and what Thomas Merton called our *secret beauty.* Merton described this secret beauty in *Conjectures of a Guilty Bystander* as being "untouched by sin and by illusion, a point of pure truth, a point or spark which belongs entirely to God . . . which is inaccessible to the fantasies of our mind or the brutalities of our own will. This little point of nothingness and of absolute poverty is the pure glory of God in us . . . It is like a pure diamond, blazing with the invisible light of heaven."[1] My teenage self was oblivious to any inner light. He was looking for light outside of himself.

Somehow I had learned to believe that self-love is possible only *if* or *when* or *after* something happens first. For example, "I'll love myself *if* my parents love me." Or "I'll love myself *when* I'm more popular." Or "I'll love myself *after* I'm famous." The list goes on. I related to self-love as an effect, not a cause. It had nothing to do with me, apparently. It was a consequence of other people's opinions and actions. It was as if they were holding my heart in their hands. How I felt about me was determined by how they felt about me. I had no idea that loving myself could be self-determined. Nor did I realize that self-love is essentially unconditional, that is, it needs no special conditions to exist.

I wish I'd continued my conversation about self-love with Adam. I could have asked him, "What is self-love?" Or even, "How do you love yourself?" But I didn't. I wasn't ready to expose my guilty secret, even though he saw it. I didn't know what self-love was, or how to do it, but I could see that it was important. Although my dad was diagnosed as an alcoholic, that wasn't his illness. His alcoholism was a symptom of his lack of self-love. Similarly, my mum was diagnosed with depression, another symptom. Her depression began in early childhood, when she felt terribly alone. Her feelings of separation—and anxious apartness—caused her to feel unloveable. She had no one to remind her of her eternal loveliness, and instead she was given prescriptions of every kind to numb the pain.

The next time I consciously thought about self-love was when I took a class on narcissism at university. A common misperception of narcissism is that narcissism is self-love, but, in truth, it's a neurosis. In Greek mythology, Narcissus was a hunter who was vain and arrogant. He saw his reflection in a pool of water and fell in love with it, not realizing it was merely an image. His self-love was only skin-deep, and it withered as his body grew old and frail. Narcissus's name is thought to derive from the Greek word *narke* (like "narcotic"), which is a "numbness" that makes you unconscious, causes you to forget, and leaves you for dead.

Narcissus didn't see the eternal loveliness of the Unconditioned Self. He was blind to the secret beauty we all share. Instead, he was fixated with his ego-self and with trying to make himself more loveable than the rest of us. The "love" he felt was only *specialness,*[2] and it cut him off from the rest of creation. Narcissistic Personality Disorder (NPD) is listed in a handbook psychologists use called *Diagnostic and Statistical Manual of Mental Disorders.* NPD is described as "a pervasive pattern of grandiosity (in fantasy or behavior), need for admiration, and lack of empathy, beginning by early adulthood."[3] Narcissism may have the look of self-love, but really it is a compensation for the basic fear of not being loveable, and, as such, it is a cause of much suffering.

What if every problem is really a symptom of a lack of love? This is the question I asked myself after I'd been practicing psychotherapy for a couple of years. As part of my practice, I ran a group therapy clinic for the National Health Service. The clinic was called Stress Busters. It was a free service held in a health center owned by the West Birmingham Health Authority.

The people who attended the clinic were referred by their doctors or self-referred. They came with their different diagnoses and difficulties, including depression, cancer, addictions, obesity, unemployment, divorce, debt, and other stresses.

Initially, I was overwhelmed by the magnitude of the problems I was presented with. It looked as if each person's problem had a separate cause and needed its own specialized treatment. That was true, of course, to an extent. However, the more we talked and got to know each other, the more we realized how much we had in common. Beneath the presenting problems was a loss of wholeness, a basic fear of not being loveable, and a wish to be happier. So we talked about being authentic, practicing self-acceptance, building self-compassion, following your joy, forgiving yourself and others, trusting yourself more, and listening to the wisdom of your heart.

I noticed how when we talked about love it made people feel better about themselves and also helped them handle their problems in a better way. Together, we helped each other recognize our blocks to love, cultivate a more loving attitude toward ourselves, and make more loving choices in our lives. Conversations about wellness and happiness had a similar effect. In one of my early books, called *Stress Busters,* I concluded, "Stress management begins with a lack of love and is complete only when there is a fullness of love."[4]

> *"Love cures people, both the ones who give it and the ones who receive it."*
>
> **Karl Menninger**

Love is a healer because it undoes the basic problem of separation and also the basic fear of not being loveable. It restores our awareness of our Unconditioned Self and our true nature. Love is, I believe, the solution to every problem. I am not the only one who thinks this way. John Welwood, a clinical psychologist and author of *Perfect Love, Imperfect Relationships,* writes, "The diagnostic manual for psychological afflictions known as the DSM [Diagnostic and Statistical Manual of Mental Disorders] might as well begin, 'Herein are described all the wretched ways people feel and behave when they do not know that they are loved.'"[5]

Gill Edwards, another clinical psychologist, makes a similar observation in her book *Wild Love*. She writes:

> Our lack of Self-love—our disconnection from Love—is the core of almost all our problems. It is the root of all our neurosis. It is the root of our relationship problems. It is the root of settling for a life of bread-and-cheese rather than inviting ourselves to the banquet. It leads to mundane lives of "quiet desperation", in the words of Thoreau—imprisoning ourselves in dull routines or stultifying relationship, or needing love (which means we won't get it), or caring for others at our own expense, or limiting ourselves to what we feel we deserve, or what others will "allow" us.[6]

When I was 25 years old, I wrote an article that I consider my first proper thesis on psychology and spirituality. It is entitled *Self-Psychology.* The central idea is the *Self Principle,* which states that *the quality of your relationship with yourself determines the quality of your relationship with everything else.* For example, how you relate to yourself influences your physical well-being, your food choices, the exercise you get, and your relationship to money. It influences your emotional well-being, the pace you set for your life, the time you make for yourself, and how loveable you feel. It also influences your spiritual well-being, your relationship to God, your creativity, and how happy you are. The better you get on with yourself, the better your life gets. Why? Because separation is not real and therefore *in any one relationship is every relationship.*

When you know that your source of love is not outside you, you don't stalk people, put them on pedestals, or turn them into idols. You treat people as equals. You don't put on a show. You express yourself without trying to win approval. You don't give love to get love. You love unconditionally, without attaching any hidden emotional invoices. You make good choices about whom to give your phone number to, whom to date, when to have sex or not, whom to be friends with, and when it's authentic to stay in a relationship or leave.

Your capacity to love yourself also influences how much you let yourself be loved by others. When you feel loveable, you don't need to put on a pleasing image to win love. Nor do you slip into a role in order to deserve love. You let love in. You are a good receiver. You aren't threatened by too much love. You are receptive to what is really happening. You recognize when you are being loved or not. You trust in love and in how loveable you are. This makes sense when you remember that we all come from the same love. In a loving relationship, "my love" and "your love," and "his love" and "her love," are all the same love, shared.

Chapter 6

Self-Love Monologue

While I was designing my first Loveability public program, I got clear that the primary focus should be on our relationship to love. I sketched out a three-day program with 12 modules, each one examining an essential facet of love. The central idea for the program was: *love is the lesson; love is the teacher.* The more you learn about love, the more it teaches you about everything else, including how to be authentic, how to be intimate, how to communicate, how to enjoy your relationships, how to forgive, and how to be truly happy.

I wanted the Loveability program to be more than just an interesting academic exercise. Love isn't just an idea; it's real. I didn't want my students to read a menu full of Greek types of love, for instance, and not actually taste anything. The Loveability program was to be an active meditation full of practical exercises to help students to recognize love and, ultimately, *to know love.* So, how do you begin to know love? The thought that kept coming to me was *To know love you must first know yourself.* As my friend Tom Carpenter once told me, "Seen rightly, 'What is love?' and 'Who am I?' are really the same question."

An inquiry into self-love happens early on in each Loveability program. I facilitate this inquiry in several ways. One way is using an exercise called the Self-Love Monologue. The brief is simple. Students pair up, each pair with a person A and a person B. In part one, person A talks about self-love for ten minutes, while person B listens without making any comments; in part two, person B speaks and person A listens. That's it. I don't give any other instructions. I simply say, "Your time starts now," and I hit the timer. The invitation is to reflect on your relationship to self-love. Ideally, I want you to share your personal experience of self-love, what you've learned, and how you practice it.

I recommend you try the Self-Love Monologue. You can do it with a friend or on your own using a voice recorder so you can listen to what you said. It's a very revealing exercise. My students often have a lot to say in the review. Many of them comment that ten minutes feels long. "Ten minutes is too long," say some. Some students report that this is the first time they've consciously thought or talked about self-love. "I had no idea where to begin" is a common comment. Another one is "I think a lot about being loved by others, but never about loving myself."

So what is self-love? This is surely one of the most important inquiries of a lifetime. I've assisted thousands of people with this inquiry over the years. To get the inquiry started, I often invite people to complete the following sentence: "To me, self-love is . . ." Some responses are playful and amusing, like "taking a bubble bath while wearing a tiara," "wearing sequins every day," and "eating organic 70 percent dark chocolate." Some responses hint at old wounds: "not being a martyr," "setting clear boundaries," and "no sex on a first date." Other responses include "getting more sleep," "doing my daily spiritual practice," and "being true to myself."

Most people cite positive actions in their initial responses to what self-love is. I did the same thing, too, when I first did a similar exercise. I don't recall exactly what I said, but I probably mentioned "my morning meditation," "playing more golf," "eating Banoffee pie," and "wearing Paul Smith socks." Responses like these, which are based on positive actions, are healthy, but they don't come close to what real self-love is. Self-love isn't just a verb;

it's deeper than that. Self-love isn't just about what you do for yourself; it's about the essence of who you are.

Self-love is, in essence, *a loving attitude from which positive actions arise that benefit you and others.* This attitude of self-love is based on an awareness of who you are and what love is. Actually, this awareness recognizes *who we all are* and what love is. That's why real self-love always benefits everyone. Love doesn't know how to single out one person and leave out another. Self-love helps you to love and be loved because it's all the same love. Seen rightly, "How do I love myself?" and "How do I love others?" are really the same question.

Staying with self-love for now, here are four key principles that are at the heart of my teaching on loving yourself.

1. Self-love is knowing who you are. Our learned self (ego, persona, self-image, call it what you like) finds it difficult to answer questions like "Who am I?" and "What do I want?" Being asked to "describe yourself" at a job interview or for a dating-agency profile, for example, can feel excruciating. The learned self has barely any true awareness. It is made up of secondhand knowledge. Its so-called learning is based on making judgments. We are conditioned to think that judging something is how you get to know it. Our learned self is simply a bag of judgments that sees nothing other than the judgments it makes. As Anthony de Mello said, "What you judge you cannot understand."[1]

> "The ego does not love you. It is unaware of who you are."
>
> **A Course in Miracles**

Self-love is what you experience when you make contact with your Unconditioned Self, which is your eternal loveliness. Self-love arises in you naturally when you see past the outer shell—your body, your ego, your personality, the face you are showing the world—and let yourself sense, feel, and recognize the spirit of who you are. The Unconditioned Self is the Self—with a capital *S*—that knows you better than your personality does. It knows you because its awareness is free of judgment. It doesn't see images. It pays no regard to any self-image you may identify with. It sees only the essence of who you are. It sees what you are made of.

2. Self-love is knowing you are made of love. Although "self-love" is made up of two separate words, self-love is not made up of two different things. Love is not a "thing" that is different from you. *Love is who you are.* I want to be really clear about this with you. I am not saying love is *in* you; I'm saying it *is* you. Similarly, love isn't a part of you; it is you. Love is your original energy. Love is the heart of who you are. Love is the consciousness of your true Self. Once again, the "you" I am referring to here is your Unconditioned Self, not the personality.

> *"Self-love is the realization that*
> *'I AM LOVE.'"*
>
> **Tom Carpenter**

Personalities don't know how to love, because they are not made up of love. Your Unconditioned Self does know how to love, because it is love. This love does not need to be manufactured by the personality. Personalities don't have to make an extra-special effort to look for love, to attract love, to win love, to be loving, and so on. All we have to do is relax. Isn't it true of everyone you know that, when they relax, they are more attractive, more fun to be with, easier to love, and also more loving? When you stop trying to be a separate personality, you can be even more of a loving presence in the world.

3. Self-love is how you really feel about yourself. People commonly experience self-love as being difficult, fragile, and too much like hard work. They avoid their own company, or feeling self-conscious, for fear of being ransacked by an unruly crowd of self-judgments. This is their experience because they are identified with their personality. However, the truth is that your Unconditioned Self, which is made of love, loves you very much.

"Your soul longs to draw you into love for yourself. When you enter your soul's affection, the torment in your life ceases," wrote John O'Donohue, the Irish Catholic priest and poet, in *Eternal*

Echoes.[2] These beautiful words are worth reading several times over. Your Unconditioned Self is a consciousness that is free of judgment, unworthiness, and lack. It is a wholly loving attitude toward yourself and everyone. Your personality is looking for love; your Unconditioned Self is love. Just stop, and breathe, and relax. Give your personality some time off and let yourself feel how much your Unconditioned Self accepts you, affirms you, and blesses you in each moment.

4. Self-love is a sacred promise kept. Self-love is a vow we make to ourselves as we enter this world. The vow is to remember our eternal loveliness and not to get lost in appearances. As children, we grow up into separate little egos, each with our own name, face, and personality. Hopefully, as we keep on growing, we realize that there is much more to us than our body, our self-image, and our story. It dawns on us that we didn't become a Self *after* we were born into this world; we *already were* a Self before we got here. The memory of that Self is what we promise to keep.

Self-love is how you are meant to feel about yourself. It is natural, not shameful. It is the key to being you. It's how you honor yourself. It reveals your secret beauty. It shows you your true value. As you commit to loving yourself more, you understand yourself better, you get what *being true to yourself* really means, and you learn how to enjoy being you. Self-love is the hidden ground that helps you to meet every challenge with a big heart. It empowers you to take your place in your life and to show the world what you are really made of.

Self-love is a commitment that says, "I will not forget who I am." It is a promise that "I will not abandon myself." It is an affirmation that "I will remember what is real." The love that is your Unconditioned Self stands by you always. Each time you are tempted to belittle yourself, to hide, to defend yourself, to be cynical, or to attack others, you can call on your Unconditioned Self to help you to choose love. Love is how we recognize ourselves and also how we recognize each other. To love somebody is a commitment that says, "I will not forget who you are," and "I will not abandon you," and "Together, we will remember what is real."

Chapter 7

Mirror Exercise

In the Loveability program we hold up a mirror to ourselves. We do this literally. In the exercise, you are given a mirror. It's quite a big mirror, the size of a *Vogue* or *GQ* magazine. You are asked to pair up with someone and to sit facing each other. Your partner holds the mirror up in front of you. For the next 15 minutes you look into the mirror and, every few seconds, say out loud, "I love myself." You are encouraged to pay attention to your responses, noticing any sensations in your body, how your heart feels, and thoughts that arise in your mind. Afterward, you hold up the mirror for your partner.

The Mirror Exercise is confronting. You may notice that just reading about it brings up all sorts of sensations, feelings, and thoughts. "That's the hardest thing I've ever done in my life," said Tim, a 46-year-old policeman, in a recent program. Some students can't do the Mirror Exercise at all. They tell me that they avoid mirrors. They say they can't get the words "I love myself" past their lips. Common responses to the exercise include lots of tears, nausea, a heavy heart, and thoughts like *This is silly* and *Surely I've done 15 minutes by now*. Curiously, by the end of the exercise most people say they feel lighter, calmer, and happier.

I remember my first time doing something like the Mirror Exercise. I was 27 years old, and I was attending a Heal Your Life workshop taught by Louise Hay. My first thought was *I can't do this.* I felt embarrassed. When I said the words *I love myself,* it sounded fake. I stopped breathing. I numbed out on myself. I prayed for time to speed up, but it seemed to slow down. Fifteen minutes can be a hell of a long time. Why did I hate this exercise so much? "The mirror isn't doing anything to you," said Louise, "so it must be you that's doing something to yourself." I didn't like hearing that. What she said was true, and I felt exposed.

The mirror wasn't judging me; I was judging me. In front of the mirror, I came face to face with my judgments about myself. The *eternal loveliness* was just a theory; all I could see were judgments. "You can't see yourself, because you're looking at your judgments," said Louise. Her words got my attention, and suddenly that made the exercise a lot more interesting. When I looked in the mirror, I thought I was looking at me, but really I was looking at my ideas about me. My judgments were looking at my judgments. This is called *projection* in psychology. As I continued with the inquiry after the workshop, I learned to suspend my judgments so I could see. What I learned was this:

> *"The real mirror is to see yourself without judgment."*
>
> **A. H. Almaas**

The self you judge is not the real self;
The self you love is the real you.

Who is judging whom? Who is the "I" that judges that "I am not enough," that fears that "I am unloveable," and that whispers, "I hate myself"? It's not your Unconditioned Self that thinks this way. It's not the *eternal loveliness* that speaks to you like this. Your Unconditioned Self existed before the first judgment was made. It continues to exist in its original innocence, even though its presence is obscured by ten thousand judgments. The Unconditioned Self may be overlooked in a mad, forgetful moment, but it is not lost. It is with you wherever you are.

Your Unconditioned Self has never judged you. It is not in its nature to do so. Can you let yourself feel that? Your Unconditioned Self has the *vision* to see who you are because it does not judge you. Self-acceptance is how your real Self feels about you. The word *acceptance* is defined in the dictionary as "belief in goodness, realness of something." To accept yourself is to make contact with and see what is real about you, not just judgments, concepts, and beliefs. If you have the courage to ask a question like "Who am I without my judgments?" you may feel disorientated initially, but soon enough you will see your true nature.

Your Unconditioned Self doesn't judge you; your ego judges you. Egos and personalities are made of judgment. Therefore, the ego's nature is to judge. Judgment is not vision. Judgment is not seeing. That's why the more you judge yourself, the less you see who you really are. Your self-judgment creates an image of yourself that declares, "I'm unloveable." By identifying with these judgments you make an *unvirtuous circle* of judgment and lovelessness that wreaks havoc

> *"Oh, my friend,*
> *All that you see of me*
> *Is just a shell,*
> *And the rest belongs*
> *to love."*
>
> **Rumi**

with your mind. Salvation comes when you drop the judgments, look at yourself through the eyes of love, and see how wholly loveable you are.

Self-Acceptance or Self-Judgment

Whenever you don't feel loveable
it's because you are judging yourself.

In each moment you are either practicing self-acceptance or you are judging yourself. You hope that you will feel loveable once there is nothing left to judge. But that isn't how reality works. For as long as you judge yourself, you will always find something more to judge. Judgment begets judgment. The unvirtuous circle of judgment and lovelessness does not stop until the last judgment. The last judgment happens when you decide to stop judging. Until then, everything about you is a target for self-judgment. The most obvious target is your body because that is what you are most identified with.

When you don't feel loveable, you pick holes in your appearance. Each time you look in the mirror, you hit yourself with thoughts like "My shape is wrong" and "I'm having a bad hair day" and "This cellulite cream is crap" and "My teeth aren't white enough." Your body is like a punching bag that takes one hit after another: "I need to dye my hair" and "My mouth is too wide" and "I wish I were two inches taller" and "I need eyedrops" and "I'm getting old" and so on. Your body has to carry the energy of these daily attacks, and you feel it mentally and emotionally. Social psychologists have done the research in the U.S. and U.K., and they tell us:

- 69 percent of men and women "often" wish they looked like someone else.[1]

- 90 percent of women feel body-image anxiety.[2]

- An estimated 19 to 30 percent of college females are diagnosed with an eating disorder.[3]

- Up to 10 million females and 1 million males struggle with eating disorders such as anorexia and bulimia.[4]

- 1 in 12 adolescents physically harms themself.[5]

The problem with judging is that judgments feel right, even when they're wrong. I repeat here, *judgment is not vision*. When you judge, you only see your judgments. That's all. If, like me, you've known someone with anorexia, and this person begs you to believe "I am too fat," then you know how off our judgments can be. I once counseled a woman diagnosed with body dysmorphic disorder, sometimes referred to as "imagined ugliness." She was five feet nine and weighed 165 pounds. The way she saw herself, she was looking at a short woman who weighed 400 pounds. Her judgments had totally distorted her vision.

The ego's version of self-acceptance is self-approval. It's nearly the same thing, except that it's completely different! Self-acceptance is the absence of judgment; self-approval *is* a judgment. My experience is that egos approve of bits and pieces of us, but never accept the whole of us. This is because the ego is not the whole of us; it's just an image. On a good day, your ego shows its approval by issuing gold stars for how good you look, or how smart you are, or how successful you are. On a bad day, your ego withdraws its approval and issues a superego report that warns that you must do better and that you must try harder.

When you judge yourself, you don't feel loveable. One solution would be to stop judging yourself and see what happens. That's not an option for the ego. What the ego does is tell you a story about an "ideal self" that is more perfect and more loveable, and it offers to build you up and accentuate the positive so that one day, maybe, you can become that ideal self. Unfortunately, this ideal self is just another image. You do your best to be more perfect, but because you are still judging yourself, you are never perfect enough. One moment, the ego is building you up; the next moment, the ego is tearing you down. It's all just an experience of judgment.

For as long as you continue to judge yourself, you go through your day as if you are on trial. You do your best to show the world your "good face," your "happy face," and your "I'm-okay face." It's hard work, though. In our relationships, we show people the bits and pieces of us that we like and hope to God they can't see the rest. We do our best to impress people. We try to look good. We are never sure, though, if people really like us or not. That's because although we might look loveable, we don't necessarily feel loveable.

> *"To see a world that doesn't judge you, you have to stop judging yourself."*
>
> **Tom Carpenter**

Our self-judging won't let us rest. When someone does love us, we can't believe our good fortune. "It's too good to be true," say our judgments. In *Essays in Love,* Alain de Botton's principal character meets Chloe, with whom he falls in love. He finds it difficult enough dealing with his love for Chloe, but he meets an even greater challenge in Chloe's love for him. At one point he confesses:

> Few things can be at once so exhilarating and so terrifying as to recognize that one is the object of another's love, for if one is not wholly convinced of one's own loveability, then receiving affection may feel like being given a great honour without quite knowing what one has done to earn it.[6]

When we judge ourselves, a shadow is cast over us. The way we treat ourselves is how we end up treating everyone else. We don't mean to do it, but it's how reality works. "She's too good for me," we say. And so we can't relax enough to really enjoy the relationship. "What have I done to deserve him?" we ask. And so we set about testing the people we love. "What's wrong with them?" we wonder. And so we start looking for flaws in others. Judging always finds something to judge, even something as lame as "They are too perfect." Neither we nor anyone else can live with our impossible judgments and ideals.

Even so, we try to justify the habit of self-judging by saying that it makes us better people. We say that if we loved ourselves unconditionally, it would prevent us from knowing "right" from "wrong" and we would somehow lose our way. As far as I can see, these theories are not based on any genuine experience or research. They are ego propaganda. The truth is that ego-personalities are afraid not to judge. "I judge, therefore I exist" is the ego's dictum. If the ego didn't judge, the ego wouldn't exist. That is the God's honest truth.

One day, when you choose, you will practice the last judgment, and when you stop judging yourself, something beautiful will happen to you. As each judgment falls away, your vision will be restored. All of a sudden, you will see your *original face*. The *eternal loveliness* of your Unconditioned Self will take the place of the *imagined ugliness* of your ego-personality. Love will reveal your *secret beauty*. Something else will happen also, which is just as wonderful. When you stop judging yourself, the habit of gratuitously judging others will also stop. *The more you love yourself, the more people feel loved by you.* It's how reality works.

Chapter 8

Childhood Messages

Love existed before the first judgment and before you doubted that you were loved and wholly loveable. Love is the memory of your wholeness. It is the Garden of Eden in which you were created. Love is the experience of total self-acceptance. It is how your Unconditioned Self originally felt about you and still does. Love is the glory you bring to earth and into childhood.[1] It is the divine inheritance you are born with, and your upbringing will encourage you either to remember your wholeness or to question it or maybe even to reject it.

Children and parents share the same basic desire, which is to love and be loved. In the beginning, infants look to their parents to mirror the love that they are. Babies want to be loved, and the parents' main focus is to love. After a while, babies show signs of also wanting to love, by making eye contact, giving away smiles (not gas-induced), and blowing

> *"Love offers us the most perfect soil for growth."*
>
> **Leo Buscaglia**

kisses. Now it's the parents' turn to be loved. This exchange of loving and being loved is essential to the growth and well-being of both child and parents.

Your parents are your first teachers. Your family is your first classroom. You take your first lessons here in everything, including love. You quickly find out about your parents' relationship to love. Every day you learn a bit more about what love means to them. Their model of love will be your first model of love. As an infant, you learn by example. Your brain is your notebook. It stores the childhood messages that are the essential data you use to make a life. You will have a relationship to these childhood messages for the rest of your days. What you choose to do with these messages has a big influence on your relationships with family, friends, lovers, and your own children, too.

In the Loveability program, I help my students investigate their childhood messages about love. The process starts with an inquiry into your relationship with your mother (or mothering influence) and your father (or fathering influence). It includes questions like:

1. Growing up, what did your mother/father teach you specifically about love?

2. As a child, how did your mother/father help you to feel loved and loveable?

3. What did you notice about how your mother/father expressed their love for each other?

4. How does your relationship with your mother/father influence your relationship to love?

5. How does your relationship with your mother/father influence how much you love yourself?

6. How does your relationship with your mother/father influence your experience of romance?

Childhood messages about love must take into account your family constellation, which includes relationships with siblings, grandparents, godparents, nannies, and family pets. When I asked my mother about her childhood, she told me she thought that Alice, the family maid, was her mother, and that Rupert, the family dog, was her main source of love. My mum was born in 1939, the last of four children, an unwanted pregnancy, her siblings much older than she. Her mother suffered from severe postnatal depression, and her father was away serving in the war. Mum often thought she was born into the wrong family. We each have a story to tell about our childhood and how loveable we felt growing up.

Childhood messages come not just from parents and family but also from your experience of school, your best friends, favorite TV shows, Barbie dolls, teenage magazines, Harry Potter, pop stars (some of whom kill themselves), football heroes, fashion models, Starsky and Hutch, Romeo and Juliet, your first crush, and also significant life events that happen along the way. By the time you're a teenager, you've gathered enough childhood messages to muddle through for the rest of your life. It's your relationship to these childhood messages (that is, what you make of them) that you take into adolescence and beyond, into romance, careers, and parenthood.

What are the key childhood messages you received about love from your upbringing? Do you know? If you were fortunate, you enjoyed a childhood full of enchantment and love. Ideally, your mother knew herself to be loveable. Your father felt good about himself, too. Your parents expressed their love for each other openly and freely. Their loveability was their legacy to you. It enabled them to love you unconditionally. They were able to create a holding environment in which you felt truly met, made safe, and provided for.

> *"Life loves you. You know how to love, and you are loveable."*
>
> **Louise Hay**

You received enough positive messages of love that you knew you were loved for who you were. Their love preserved in you a *basic trust* in the goodness of love and in your own loveability.

Most of us grew up with parents who were still learning about their own loveability. They were working this out in their relationship with each other, and also with us. We were part of each other's curriculum on love. In my childhood, I felt loved by my parents *most* of the time. However, my mum's episodes of depression, which left her bedridden for months on end, and my father's secret refuge with alcohol definitely cast a shadow. The family home we lived in for 14 years was called *Shadows*. There were plenty of shadows in our family story, which I had to revisit later on. I even ended up teaching a class on Shadow Psychology for ten years at The Interfaith Seminary.[2]

In the Loveability program I ask my students, "Would you have had a happier childhood if your mother and father had loved themselves more?" I learned this question from Cheryl Richardson, author of *The Art of Extreme Self-Care*.[3] In a group of 100 people, 99 people raise their hand as a "yes" to this question. Most of these people are parents themselves. So the next obvious question is "Would your children have a happier upbringing if you loved yourself more?" The penny drops, hopefully. As parents, we are always trying to love our children the best we can. The curriculum for this lasts a lifetime, and the curriculum includes loving ourselves.

Our upbringing isn't just about our parents. I remember my loveability was tested by the arrival of my younger brother, David. David was born one week after my fourth birthday. "He's your birthday present," I was told. David was a cute, loveable teddy bear of a boy. He was so lovely that I wanted to exchange him for a bike or some other present. Suddenly, life wasn't so fair. "Why am I not enough?" "Why does he get all the attention?" Another major test to my loveability was being bullied at school. My mum and dad came to my rescue, but there were still scars that needed to be healed.

Most childhoods are full of mixed messages about love. We were loved but not unconditionally. We soon got the message of *conditional love* from parents, teachers, and friends, and the message was: "You are loveable if . . ." and "You are loveable when . . ." Conditional love isn't freely given; it has to be earned, deserved, and won. Our task was to crack the code to conditional love. We learned, for instance, that our mother gave us more smiles when we behaved well, and our father gave us his attention when we got good grades in school, and our best friend liked us if we agreed with him, and our teachers gave us gold stars for following the rules.

What's especially confusing for a child is that the rules of conditional love vary with each person. There are no standard rules. You have to work them out with each parent, each teacher, each friend, and the rest of the world after that. It was inevitable that you would make mistakes and suffer the consequences. The worst thing my mum and dad could ever say to me was "We are so disappointed in you." They had only to give me a certain look with their eyes, and I'd collapse into a heap of shame. The slightest hint of rejection from my parents felt unbearable. I would do anything so as not to be rejected.

Every child has to learn to adapt him- or herself in order to meet the requirements of conditional love. Some of this adaptation is healthy. It really is a good idea not to bite people, to learn how to share, to brush your teeth, and to say sorry when you set off a stink bomb under your brother's bed. Being adaptive is healthy and necessary, but too much adaptation (brought on by too many conditions of love) can cause us to abandon our authentic self and replace it with a more pleasing *image* that hopefully gets us out of trouble and wins us more love. This is how we first experience a *loss of being* and how our Unconditioned Self is replaced by a persona and an act.

Sadly, the mixed messages of childhood are sometimes accompanied by terrible traumas. The death of a parent or a sibling can leave a child feeling like love no longer exists for him or her. A child whose parents separate and/or divorce often feels torn in two. Too many children experience abuse at the hands of their parents and other authority figures. The abuse can take many forms, including physical harm, emotional attacks, and sexual abuse. Many children also grow up in poverty, with sickness, and in war zones. Whatever the worst is that you can imagine, some children have had it worse.

With conditional love, we are not loved for who we are; we are loved for how we behave. So we become little actors, and we take on childhood roles in order to survive and to feel okay about ourselves. We wear these childhood roles either lightly like a loose garment or heavily like a suit of armor, depending on our childhood messages and our reaction to them. These roles are significant because they show up later in our romantic relationships and also our relationships with friends, colleagues, and, of course, our children. They can be a major challenge and/or block to loving and being loved. Here are some classic examples of childhood roles:

1 **The Good Child:** who believes "When I am good, I am loveable." He behaves like a good little adult who is neat and tidy, gets things right, and is never a nuisance. When you believe that "being good" equals "being loveable," you tell yourself, "I must always be on good behavior." In adulthood, you show up as the "good friend," the "good partner," and the "good parent." Wanting to be a good person is natural; telling yourself you must always be good so as to deserve love is a problem. The effort to be good hides a fear that "I am not good enough." You confuse love with approval. You are afraid that if you put one bad foot forward it will be unforgivable.

2 **The Helping Child:** who believes "If I help you, I will be loved." She behaves like a little angel or nurse who puts everyone else first and is always on hand to make everything better. When you show up in the role of "the helper," you are forever helping others, but you never let yourself be helped. You attract friendships in which you position yourself as "the giver" and they have to be "the receiver." No wonder, then, that you end up exhausted and in sacrifice. Similarly, in romance, you attract people you hope to save in some way. The person who needs to be saved is you. Wanting to help people is an expression of love; believing you always have to be "the helper" is really a call for love.

3 **The Star Child:** who believes "When I am outstanding, I am loveable." He works hard to make his parents proud, to win admiration, and to enjoy the applause. When you believe that only your best self is loveable, you force yourself to be on your best behavior as often as possible. According to you, love is an Oscar, and you need to give your best performance to win it. Your best efforts are a compensation for feeling unworthy. The basic fear "I am not loveable" does not trust that the authentic you—the natural you—is even more loveable than the "you" that's trying so hard to be a "great parent," a "model wife," and so on.

6 **The Happy Child:** who believes "When I'm happy, I'm more loveable." She adopts a bouncy, positive demeanor so as to convince everyone that she is "A-OK," never sad, angry, or worried. For example, Jo is in her late 20s. She's a stand-up comedian. Her mother has been diagnosed with bipolar disorder, commonly known as manic depression. Growing up, comedy was Jo's lifeline. It helped her to keep cheerful and stay positive. She came to the Loveability program because she realized that her be-happy attitude was blocking real intimacy in her relationships. Her fear was that unhappiness is unacceptable and that it drives love away. "I don't want to be a smiley face anymore," she said. "I want to love all of me, and I want others to love all of me, too."

4 **The Melancholy Child:** who believes "When I'm unhappy, I get more love." She notices that her parents put her first when she cries, when she's ill, and when she withdraws into herself. Her melancholy gets her the attention she craves. It helps her to be seen, even though it is just an act. She feels loved, even if the attention she gets isn't real love. In romance, the melancholy adult fantasizes about being rescued by a hero. The trouble is, it's hard to believe in heroes or in love when you stand in a well of melancholy all day long. In the melancholy role, you are afraid to be happy because you fear that if all is well, you won't get attention and love. It's impossible to rescue someone who is afraid of happiness.

8 **The Independent Child:** who believes "When I'm independent, I can't be hurt." He acts like a good little soldier who tries to be strong, grown up, and self-contained. William is the perfect example. His father left home when William was four years old. He never saw his dad again. William's mother had no money or support, and she had to place him in an orphanage. William's brother was also sent away to live with an uncle and aunt. William's mother managed to reunite the family six years later. When William came into the Loveability program, he told the group, "Being independent saved me back then, but now I can see that my independence is a block to trusting in love and letting myself be loved." Similar roles include the Loner and the Misfit.

7 **The Rebel Child:** who believes "I'm unloveable anyway." She acts like a rebel because she doesn't feel loved. The rebellion is a call for love that also pushes love away. Like the Independent Child, the Rebel Child is reacting to a wound and to fear. Other similar roles include the Maverick Child and the Difficult Child. *To rebel* is not a problem, but to *be a rebel* does cause problems, especially in relationships and in love. Rebels tend to be attracted to drama. They like to fight against something. They date the wrong types. They have a tragic view of love because of how they see themselves. Love is dangerous for a rebel because love is surrender. A rebel cannot survive love.

5 **The Genius Child:** who believes "If I know how, I can be loved." Being competent, knowing how things work, excelling at something helps this child to find his place in the world. For example, Tony is a professor of medicine at a university in England. He attended a public program of mine called *Authentic Success*. He told the group that he had doubts about staying in medicine. When I asked him why he became a doctor, he said, "I fell in love with a girl when I was eleven years old and I knew for sure that she wouldn't

love me unless I was brilliant at something." Tony was currently working on a second Ph.D., and he was still looking for love.

9 **The Peaceful Child:** who believes "When you feel loved, I feel loveable." She does whatever she can not to rock the boat, not to be a burden, and not to upset anyone. The Peacemakers, as these types are called, love to feel harmony and oneness in relationships. They will do whatever it takes to preserve some semblance of union, even if that means leaving themselves out. A similar role to the Peaceful Child is the Invisible Child. In this role, the fear is "If I get too involved it may upset the peace." Therefore, "I will not ask for anything for myself." However, there cannot be peace if you are missing. The truth is that your loving presence is the key to peace on earth.

Chapter 9

Your Love Story

You emerge from your childhood with a story to tell. It's a story about who you are, what has happened to you, and how loveable you feel. This is how your love story begins. You are the central character, the protagonist. Other characters, such as the antagonist or the object of your love play into the basic plot of your story. Sometimes you play the hero or heroine; other times you play the villain or the victim, for instance. You play many parts, not just in your own story but in others' stories, too. Your story is what you take into the world. It's the story you project onto your romances, in your marriage, and in raising your own family.

We are all storytellers. We start telling stories from a young age. My daughter, Bo, is full of stories. Some of her stories are made up. They are so convincing that she doesn't always know the difference between something real or imagined. Most of her stories are a commentary on what's happening. "You don't love me!" shouts Bo when I say, "Let's not eat ice cream for breakfast." That's her story. "That's so unfair," she says when I don't let her drive the car. That's her story. "That's so rude," she yells when I suggest playing a game together instead of watching TV. And at nighttime, when we all lie in bed together, Bo will say, "Mummy. Daddy. Please tell me a story about when you were young."

Storytelling is always subjective. It's your version of what happened, and if anyone else was involved, they have their version, too. Your story and their story might be completely different even though they are based on the same events. When my brother, David, and I talk about our childhood, and all that happened, and the effect it had on us, Hollie says it often sounds like we grew up in two different families. We have our own stories about which one of us Dad loved the most, who was Mum's favorite, who never got told off, and who had it the worst. Sometimes we can't even agree on facts like dates or on the sequence of specific events. Fortunately for us, we do both love being each other's brother.

Stories are full of meaning. They are based on events and also on the meaning we give the events. The meaningful part of the story is our interpretation of what happened. It's the most significant part, because after the events are finished, we carry the meaning forward, which keeps our story alive. This is also how old stories get projected onto present relationships. For example, Alice, a 30-year-old woman, came to see me for counseling. She told me, "I'm hopeless at relationships because I have abandonment issues." Alice's father died when she was three years old. "He abandoned me," she told me. That was the meaning she gave to her father's death. That was her story, and she had played it out in her relationships with men ever since.

Stories don't just happen to us. We play our part too. We are born into this world with our own disposition and temperament, and this influences our perception (the way we see things) and our interpretation (the meaning we give things) of what happens. Personalities are conceived before birth. Mothers get to know their babies as they carry them in their wombs. We don't arrive as blank slates. We have our preferences. We may attach ourselves to one parent, reject the other, be ambivalent toward both, and frequently change our mind about who is our favorite. We go about our life in our own way right from the start. It's important that we take this into account when we examine our story about love and our loveability.

The basic truth is that you are loved and wholly loveable. This basic truth is the memory of your wholeness. It is the awareness of your Unconditioned Self. It is the Original Blessing. It is your eternal loveliness. When you remember this basic truth, you declare with confidence, "I am loved for who I am." You experience real self-acceptance, and so the message you give yourself is "I am loveable." This is not ego inflation. You are not saying that you're more loveable than others. You don't tell yourself you have to be something *more* or *better* or *different*. You don't need to put on a face, wear a pleasing image, or play a role. You trust that *being yourself* is the key to loving and being loved.

We start to tell stories about ourselves when we forget the basic truth. These stories are normally based on a basic fear, and that fear is "I am not loveable." This basic fear is the central judgment that our personality wrestles with. It is the root of all fear. It is a rejection of our wholeness. It is the fall from grace. John Steinbeck wrote in *East of Eden:* "The greatest terror a child can have is that he is not loved, and rejection is the hell he fears. I think everyone in the world to a large or small extent has felt rejection. And with rejection comes anger, and with anger some kind of crime in revenge for the rejection, and with the crime, guilt—and there is the story of mankind."[1]

The basic fear of "I am not loveable" is our *primal lie* about ourselves.[2] It feeds our negative self-concepts. It shows us an unloveable self-image. It convinces us to abandon our authentic nature and to adopt a role that will hopefully save us from more rejection. This basic fear is the only fear there is. In order to preserve itself, it splits itself up into presenting fears (or secondary fears), which it then hides behind. These presenting fears may look different, but they are all clustered around the same basic fear of "I am not loveable." Here are two common examples of these secondary fears:

> **"I am not enough."** When you believe "I am not loveable," you lose sight of who you are. The knowledge of your wholeness is obscured by perceptions of lack. When you look in the mirror you see a person who is not

beautiful enough, attractive enough, smart enough, successful enough, or abundant enough. Vision is replaced with judging. You think you understand yourself only too well, but you are not really seeing yourself. All you are seeing is the projection of your judgments.

When you judge yourself, the personality compares itself negatively with others. You keep trying to change yourself into something better, but nothing really changes because you haven't stopped telling yourself, "I am not loveable." No amount of makeovers or reinvention or new beauty secrets seems to do the trick. Even when you are in a dream relationship and you appear to have it all, it still feels like something is missing. Of course, what's really missing is more of the real you. Nothing really changes until you are willing to see the real you.

"I'm too much." When you tell yourself, "I am unloveable," you are rejecting yourself, and that's what makes you afraid of being rejected by everyone else, too. To compensate, you try to "be enough" but not "too much." The fear that "I am too much" also splits itself off into more fears, like "I'm too big for you" or "I'm too difficult to be with" or "I am too independent" or "I am too much of a free spirit." You do your best to tone yourself down, to be more palatable, and to not to come on too strong. You are even willing to play small if it means not being rejected again.

I met Susan at a dinner in London celebrating historic vintages of wine from the Mouton Rothschild estate. Susan was in her early 50s, the CEO of her own company, and, like me, a wine lover. As the wine flowed, Susan told me, "Men are scared of me." When I asked her why, she said, "I'm too powerful." She also said, "Men don't like rich women." That was her story. I asked her if she got scared of men who weren't scared of her. "All men are weak," she said. That was fear speaking. Her complaint about men was really her defense against men. It was her way of rejecting others before she could be rejected by them.

The basic fear "I am not loveable" can play itself out in so many ways. Other common secondary fears include:

"There is something wrong with me."

"I am not wanted."

"I am not seen."

"I am not understood."

"I am incapable."

"I am not safe."

"I am not interesting."

"I am all alone."

"I don't matter."

The basic fear is just a story. It feels real because you have learned to identify with it. "It's my story," says the ego. "It's how I recognize myself, and how I know I exist." When you are identified with a story, you keep creating the story. How so? You date people who match your level of self-esteem. You are attracted to people who mirror your beliefs about yourself. You train your friends to treat you the way you treat yourself. You let others do to you what you are already doing to yourself. These people are the cast in your story. They show up and behave in ways that fit with your story about you and about love.

Can you see what's really happening here? You are the actor in your own story, but you are acting as if your story about you is a biography, not an autobiography.

By telling yourself *I am unloveable,* you let your ego-personality write your life story for you. You have forgotten your basic truth (I am loveable), and so you have forgotten that your Unconditioned Self can also help to write, direct, and star in your story. The story of your life cannot change by itself. It changes only as you change your mind about yourself. This change of mind begins with a willingness to start again.

Even if your parents weren't perfect, and even if you weren't raised with unconditional love, and even if your history is full of heartache, the truth remains that *whether someone loves you or not has no bearing on how loveable you really are.* Your childhood is not the last chapter in your story. Your first love is not your only love. Your greatest heartache is not the whole story of your life. Your parents are not God. An unhappy past, no matter how terrible, is not a reason to say "I am not loveable," nor is it a reason to stop loving yourself. Actually, it is a reason to love yourself more.

You can only be held back by your past if you use it to reject yourself in the present.

Your life is a love story. It is the story of how much you are willing to love yourself so that you can love others and be loved. Your story looks like a separate story from everyone else's, but this is part of the story. Each of our love stories looks different, but really the storyline is the same. We are the Beloved in search of love. Love is who we are. We search for love because we want an experience of the basic truth, which is at the heart of our Unconditioned Self. The drama begins when we encounter the basic fear and we identify with it. Love is what saves us in the end.

The willingness to love yourself again begins with an act of courage and imagination. Perhaps you get out a journal and you write down a sentence that begins, *If I really loved myself I would . . .* Or another sentence might begin with *One way I could love myself more is . . .* You probably notice some resistance at first. This resistance is an expression of the basic fear "I am not loveable." This fear deserves your compassion. It is a call for love. You've been waiting for a long time to find someone who will love you so that you will love yourself again. Maybe that person is you.

In my own story about learning to love myself, I found a prayer. It's a prayer that I wrote about in my book *Happiness NOW!* I found this prayer when I was 30 years old. It was unlike any prayer I had ever seen before. It was a prayer that helped me to realize the difference between vision and judgment, knowledge and perception, God and ego. I think of this prayer as an angel that reintroduced me to the Unconditioned Self and to the basic truth "We are all loveable." A Benedictine nun named Macrina Wiederkehr created this prayer. It goes like this:

O God, help me to believe the truth about myself
no matter how beautiful it is!
Amen.[3]

PART III

Love Has No Conditions

Sam is an actor. He is in his early 20s. He lives in Notting Hill, London, and also in Venice Beach, Los Angeles. We first met at one of my public programs called "Love's Philosophy," which explores the relationship between spiritual and romantic love. After that, Sam signed up for some occasional one-to-one coaching sessions with me. In the short time I've known Sam, about three years, he has fallen in love at least six times. On each occasion he believed he'd met "the One," as he put it. Now, the latest love of his life had left him, and Sam was distraught again. We set up an appointment to meet.

"I thought she was 'the One,'" said Sam, hanging his head down over his heart.

"Why was she 'the One'?" I asked.

"It felt so right," he replied.

"How so?"

"She made me feel so good about myself."

"How did she do that?" I asked.

"She was also so beautiful."

"Really," I said.

"She was a model, you know," said Sam.

Our conversation was disjointed. Sam barely registered my questions. He was in a lot of pain. Tears fell into his hands. He didn't want a tissue. Occasionally, his body shuddered from head to toe, as if it were trying to shake something off itself. I'd seen Sam this way before. He was always so "up" when he met a new girl, and so "down" on himself when it didn't work out. "I'm confused, boss," he said, over and over again. Much of what Sam said wasn't spoken directly to me. It was like he was talking to himself, or to his mother (who had died on the day of his eighth birthday), or to God, maybe. At one point he said, "All I want is to love somebody enough that they don't leave."

"How did you meet her?" I asked.

"I think I manifested her," said Sam.

"How did you do that?"

"I went to a Law of Attraction seminar in L.A.," he told me.

"What happens at one of those?"

"First, you make a picture of your ideal mate, and then you affirm that she exists, and then you ask the universe to send her to you."

"And the universe delivers the pizza," I said.

"I guess so," said Sam, who, like me, wasn't sure where the pizza comment had come from.

When I asked Sam about the picture he had made, he pulled out a folded piece of white paper from his wallet, opened it up, and read to me a wish list that included physical features like "dark hair," "green eyes," "thin lips," "nice smile," "perfect body," "Italian or Italian-looking," and also other qualities like "artistic," "spiritual," "successful," and "good sense of humor." When he finished, he gave me the list to look at. Alongside the list was a cutout magazine photo of the actress Demi Moore. At the top of the page, Sam had written "THE ONE" in big, bold capital letters.

The day after the Law of Attraction seminar, Sam boarded a British Airways evening flight from LAX to Heathrow. As he was about to take his seat in Premium Economy, a flight attendant told him he was to be upgraded to Club World, business class. His new seat was 3A. Sitting in seat 3B was the model (I don't recall Sam giving me her name). Sam told me how they got talking, and that they talked all through the night, with no sleep, until their plane parked at its gate at Terminal 5. "She was everything on my list," said Sam, who was clearly impressed with the universe.

Their first date "on the ground," as Sam put it, was at The Ivy restaurant, in London's West End.

"It was perfect," said Sam.

"How so?"

"She looked stunning. Everyone noticed us. We were such a good fit," he said. "We laughed and talked all evening. The sommelier even poured us a glass of complimentary champagne at the end of the night, and suggested we make a toast to 'young love.'"

"It must have felt like you were on a film set," I said.

"Exactly," said Sam, "and we fell in love that night, or so I thought."

Later, Sam took the model back to his flat in Notting Hill. It was their second night together, if you include the plane trip, and once again they got no sleep. Sam described the chemistry between them as "insane" and "the best ever."

"So what happened on your second date?" I asked.

"I missed it," said Sam.

"How so?"

"Well, after our first proper night together," explained Sam, "I realized that she had the most perfect body. She's a model, remember."

"Yeah, I remember," I said.

"Well, compared to her, I'm way out of shape," he said. "So I signed up at the local gym and started working out. I set myself a goal of 1,000 daily sit-ups and 500 daily push-ups. Anyway, two hours before our second date I collapsed in the gym with a suspected hernia. I called her from the locker room and told her I had to cancel."

"Did you tell her what had happened?" I asked.

"No way," said Sam.

"That's a pity," I said.

"Why?"

"Well, you could have found out if she had a sense of humor."

Sam and the model met up every few days over the next two months. It was all going so well.

"And then I ruined it," said Sam.

"How did you do that?" I asked.

"I'm not exactly sure."

"Give me something specific," I pressed him.

"I started feeling not good enough," said Sam. "She's a model. She's really successful. She earns more money than I do. Most of her friends are famous. I guess I began to doubt myself."

"Did you tell her any of this?"

"No way," said Sam.

After two months, the model went away to Florence for a long weekend for a photo shoot.

"We started to misfire after that," said Sam.

"How so?"

"We just cooled off, I guess."

"Why?"

"Something was missing, I guess."

"What was that?" I asked.

"I think she withdrew from me," said Sam.

"Or maybe you withdrew from her," I said.

"Maybe."

"And did you talk about this?" I asked.

"No way," said Sam.

Sam and the model hadn't spoken for eight days, which was a sure sign in Sam's mind that the romance was over. When I suggested that Sam call her, he told me that wasn't a good idea.

"She's gone," he said.

"I'm sorry," I said.

"Me too," said Sam.

"Are you really sure you were both in love?"

"Yeah, I thought so," said Sam. "But now I'm not sure if I've ever been in love."

"That must be very confusing," I said.

"Yeah, you bet."

Sam fell silent. He looked like he was replaying in his mind the events of the past three months. Putting all the pieces together. Trying to understand what had happened. Feeling the grief of another love lost.

"Why did she leave me?" he asked at last, shaking his head.

"You could ask her, you know," I suggested.

"What went wrong?"

"Do you know, Sam?"

Sam drew a heavy breath into his chest. He didn't answer my question; instead he came back with a question of his own.

"How do you know if someone really loves you, and if you really love them?"

"Those are good questions, Sam," I said.

"I want answers, Doc," he said, as he lifted his gaze from the floor. "And I need them quick, before I fall in love again."

Like Sam, my early romances were full of infatuation and fantasy. I carried around a deep yearning to fall in love. I wanted it more than anything, even though I had no idea what love was. As the old saying goes, *I was in love with the idea of being in love.* Some of my friends fell in love with lots of girls. I was waiting for "my love" to show up. In the meantime, rather than think seriously about love, I carried on learning the guitar, playing cricket, hanging out with the cool crowd, and generally putting myself out there.

> *"Love waits on welcome, not on time."*
>
> **A Course in Miracles**

Sam had thought about love. He was a keen student of Buddhism. He talked openly about his high regard for Jesus, and Jesus's teaching on forgiveness. When in L.A., he attended a study group for *A Course in Miracles.* When in London, he would keep Monday nights free to go to lectures on spirituality hosted by Alternatives, at St. James's Church, in Piccadilly.[1] Intellectually, Sam understood that love is bigger than romance. He could tell you that romance doesn't create love, but rather *love is what creates romance.* And yet when it came to romance he was always *falling in love,* but he was not able to enjoy the grace and happiness of *being in love.*

Loveability is what makes romance possible. When you know you are loveable and you remember your *eternal loveliness,* you are attractive in the highest sense. Sam thought that the Law of Attraction was simply about thinking positive thoughts and saying happy affirmations, but that's not the heart of it. The heart of the Law of Attraction starts with how you see yourself. *Literally, you attract what you identify with.* Therefore, if you feel loveable, you attract loving relationships, because that's what you relate to. If you don't feel loveable, you attract something that isn't love, because that's what you relate to.

> **It's the love you feel inside yourself**
> **that helps you to know if the love you**
> **have with someone is real or not.**

Chapter 10

Is This Love?

We are obsessed in our society with falling in love. It is a social fever that provokes a delirium in us from a young age. Cast your mind back to your school days. Do you remember how old you were when you and your friends first talked about boyfriends and girlfriends? Do you remember how the conversation went? Was it full of phrases like "He's cute" and "She's cool" and "He's staring at you" and "She fancies you"? I assume you didn't talk much about agape or loving kindness, unless, that is, you grew up in a monastery or an ashram. To the very young, love is only about falling in love.

Just the other day, my daughter Bo, who has just turned five years old, ran up to me all excited and out of breath. She'd been on her first play-date with our next-door neighbor's son, Jonathan, who is seven years old. She jumped onto my lap and whispered into my ear, "Daddy, I really like Jonathan. He doesn't know it yet, but I think he might be my boyfriend." After that, Bo wore her best dresses, tried on a brand new laugh, put on a super-happy voice, and hung over the garden fence for hours waiting for Jonathan to make an appearance. Jonathan really likes Bo, but he likes football more. And, thankfully, Bo is too full of love and excited about life to have let it get her down for long.

Imagine what a difference it would make to children's lives if they were introduced to their eternal loveliness before they started obsessing about falling in love. Consider for a moment how much pain and confusion you'd have been saved from if someone had talked to you about unconditional love before you got swept away with the birds and the bees. When you remember that you are made of love, and that you are deeply loveable, you can show up unconditionally everywhere. The more unconditional we are with each other, the more we experience real love in our family, with our friends, and, of course, in our romances.

The early obsession with falling in love is a sign that we have already started to doubt our own loveability. By falling in love with someone, we hope we will remember how loveable we are. We hope someone will catch our fall, in the fall from grace, and thereby save us from the basic fear that "I am not loveable." Much of the desire to fall in love is about being loved rather than being loving. As J. Krishnamurti wrote, "You want to be loved because you do not love; but the moment you love, it is finished, you are no longer inquiring whether or not somebody loves you."[1]

Like Sam, we may fall in love many times over before we decide to stop falling and to start thinking about what real love is. Getting clear on what love is—unconditional love, specifically—may mean that you have to unlearn a lot of conditioning acquired from parents, from school friends, from sexy celebrities, from boyfriends and girlfriends, and from society in general. What looks and feels like love often isn't love at all. As you embrace your loveability, you begin to see clearly again what love is. Similarly, as you learn to love others unconditionally, you also let yourself be unconditionally loved.

So what is unconditional love? And how do you know if someone really loves you, and if you really love them? Here are five ideas that I teach in the Loveability program that are relevant to every form of relationship, including romances.

1. Love is not an act. One of the joys of real friendship and true love is that we can both be our real selves in each other's company. Neither of us has to put on a face in order to be loved. We don't always have to be on our best behavior with each other. We don't need to put on a performance by trying to look good, be positive, be strong, or be happy all the time. Our love for each other is not about approval; it's about acceptance. I love you and you love me

> *"When you love someone, you love the person as they are, and not as you'd like them to be."*
>
> **Leo Tolstoy**

because we both really "get" each other. We both get a kick out of how much we enjoy each other exactly as we are.

Unconditional love creates a holding environment in a relationship that makes it safe for you to be yourself. Love is not an audition. You don't have to turn yourself into a pleasing image in order to get the part. You don't have to be an attractive package. You don't have to be a beautiful version of yourself all the time. You don't have to dress yourself up or tone yourself down. You aren't trying to win a place in each other's hearts. You live in each other's hearts already. Unconditional love isn't about making the right impression; it's about intimacy. You don't have to act. You don't have to hide. You don't have to lie. Honesty is not a threat to unconditional love.

As we get to know each other, we discover that we have many similar tastes, shared interests, and matching values. No wonder we feel such an affinity toward each other. That said, there is also space in our relationship for individuality, diversity, and eccentricity. Our love for each other is big enough to honor our differences. Neither of us has to be a chameleon, a photocopy, or a twin. We are extensions of each other, but not replicas. We are One, but we don't have to be exactly the same. In love, we respect that, for instance:

- We don't both have to be extroverts.

- We don't both have to be vegans.

- We don't have to like the same movies.

- We don't have to have the same friends.

- We don't have to hold identical points of view.

- We don't have to follow the same career paths.

- We don't have to live our lives exactly the same way.

- We don't both have to be Jews, or Christians, or Muslims.

- We don't have to have the same color skin.

You know you love someone when you can honestly say that you don't need them to change before you love them more. That said, we are changed by unconditional love. The change that happens is organic and natural. We stop being an image, and we become more real. "Love takes off masks that we fear we cannot live without and know we cannot live within," wrote the author James Baldwin.[2] Good impressions give way to genuine intimacy. A deep acceptance of each other helps to heal the last remnants of self-rejection. Our unconditional love for each other helps us both to grow into who we really are. The change we both witness is a mark of evolution and a miracle of love.

2. Love is not a bargain. I know it's common to talk about giving and receiving in relationships, and how both parties should make equal deposits into the "love bank." This sort of talk is typical of how egos make agreements and contracts with each other. Invariably, both egos end up filing separate complaints about giving too much love or not getting enough love. With unconditional love, giving and receiving are experienced in a different light. Love is a way of being; it is not a thing to give away. Love is an attitude; it is not a currency you buy things with. In love, nothing is taken and nothing is

> *"True love begins when nothing is looked for in return."*
>
> **Antoine de Saint-Exupéry**

lost, because love is who you are, and love extends itself without ever leaving its source.

Love does not make deals. Love does not say, "I will give you love, but first you must give me something else." Love cannot be bought. You cannot buy love with sex, for instance. If ever someone appears to be offering you love in return for sex, you can be sure that this love is a fake. Love cannot be sold. It is not love when a friend says, "Agree with me and I will like you," or when a parent says, "Do as I say and you have my approval," or when a lover says, "Give me what I want and I will be happy." These ultimatums deal in fear and guilt, not love. In love, you can ask each other for anything, but you demand nothing of each other. Love makes no demands.

All this talk about giving love and receiving love can make it sound like love can only be found in a marketplace. Love is not for sale. If you look with your heart, you will see that it costs you nothing to give love, because giving love is really just being loving. Similarly, there is not a price to pay when receiving love, because your receptiveness is just another aspect of being loving. When you are being loving, you are not making a purchase. You are not giving away an arm or a leg; you are simply showing each other how you really feel. This is why there is no loss in love. And because there is no loss, and no invoices and receipts, there is never any debt to settle.

I once found a most beautiful description of unconditional love in a poem by Hafiz (and translator Daniel Ladinsky) called "The Sun Never Says." It reads:

> **Even after all this time,**
> **The sun never says to the earth:**
> **"You owe me!"**
>
> **Look what happens with**
> **A love like that!**
> **It lights the whole sky!**[3]

3. Love is not idolatry. When I was 11 years old, I went to the Henry Beaufort School. There were 1,000 pupils at my new school, compared with only 75 pupils in my previous one. I was daunted by the size of everything and felt very lonely. I soon learned that the coolest boy in my year was Mike Furber. No one was more popular than Mike. Mike ended up as captain of the football team, the hockey team, and the rugby team. The only team he wasn't captain of was the cricket team, and that's because I was the captain of the cricket team. Mike Furber and I became best friends. Being Mike's best friend was wonderful and awful. I loved it and I hated it. Mike was so cool, but he was also moody. I allowed his moods to get the better of me. So, when Mike liked me, I liked me; but when Mike didn't like me, I didn't like me, and when Mike ignored me, I hated me.

I was too young to know what was happening at the time, but later I realized that what I'd done was to make Mike Furber into an idol. When Mike wanted to be my best friend, I couldn't believe my good fortune. I felt like I'd won the jackpot, yet I was amazed that there was even a ticket with my name on it. I didn't feel equal to Mike. My lack of self-love made me turn Mike into an idol and into a source of love. Whenever you make a person into a source of love—be it a best friend, a parent, a lover, a child—that person also becomes a source of fear, unhappiness, and suffering. I'm happy to say that Mike Furber and I are still friends. I'll send him a copy of this book when it's finished, and I'll put a note inside telling him to read this page. I know I'll a get phone call when he does.

Love exists only between equals, because love recognizes everyone as equals. Therefore, in love no one is better than anyone else, no one is superior or inferior, and no one is more loveable. We are equals because we are made of the same love. There are not different grades of love. When you don't feel equal, you give yourself away. And then you take on a role in the relationship such as the sidekick, the martyr, the poor relation, the servant, the helper, the doormat, the cheerleader, or the chief polisher of pedestals. Roles prevent you from feeling equal. They block intimacy. They conceal dishonesty. You feel unloveable.

In love, we raise each other up, without one ending up higher than the other. Love brings out the best in both of us, not just in one of us. If one of us gives ourself away, then we also give our power away, and this is what causes power struggles in relationships. Power struggles happen because we think we are both separate and different from each other. We forget that we are made of the same love and that we both share the same basic interest, which is *to love and be loved*. Power struggles cause all sorts of fights in relationships. And the mind-set that puts people on pedestals also blows up pedestals. It's only when you resume an equal position that you can take responsibility for your part in a relationship and be a more loving person.

> *"Recognize all whom you see as brothers, because only equals are at peace."*
>
> **A Course in Miracles**

4. Love is not special. If someone says to you, "I've been saving all my love for you," I recommend you turn around and run for your life. Why? Well, it sounds like they've never loved someone before. That means they must be completely out of touch with love. It also means that you must be their experiment. Good luck with that! I know it sounds romantic to say things like "You are the only one I've ever loved" and "You are my one true love," but honestly that is not how unconditional love expresses itself. The goal of love is not just to love one person; it is to love everyone. Indeed, it is only when you are willing to love everyone that you will be able to love someone.

Looking for "the One," as my client Sam put it, creates what is described in *A Course of Miracles* as an "endless, unrewarding chain of special relationships."[4] The term *special relationships* refers to relationships that see people as objects of love. The goal of a special relationship is to milk as much love as possible from your holy cow. The word *special* signifies an attempt to separate your holy cow from the herd so that you can live in a little field together somewhere that is fenced off from the rest of the world. This is how you split yourself off from oneness. You end up as an alienated couple. It is egoism *à deux*.[5] You operate as a closed system, and one day you realize you are closed off from love.

Love is not exclusive. In relationships, you can make exclusive agreements. For example, in romance you can agree to monogamous sex; in friendship you can share certain confidences; and in business you can create sole partnerships. However, in love you cannot attempt to love each other exclusively and succeed in creating a loving relationship. Saying "I love you above all others" might seem like a nice idea, but, actually, it is impossible. *You can only love someone as much as you are willing to love everyone.* This is how true love works. Making someone your special love object, your holy cow, doesn't create love; rather, it leads to dependency, possessiveness, jealousy, neurosis, and ten thousand other forms of fear.

> *"As our love for our partner increases, so will our love for everyone increase."*
>
> **Chuck Spezzano**

**When you love someone, you want
everyone else to love them too.
You are happy for them to experience the
joy of loving and being loved by everyone.**

5. Love is not selfish. In his book *The Power of Unconditional Love,* Ken Keyes, Jr., advises us, "As you consider going into a relationship, look deeply into your heart and mind to discover your level of commitment to the other person's well-being."[6]

In the dance of romantic love, in particular, love is always love, but sometimes other characters like lust and infatuation masquerade as love. This can cause a lot of confusion and pain. I am often asked how you can tell the difference between lust, infatuation, and love. Here's what I say:

- **Lust is physical desire.** It is full of physical fireworks. All you want from your "love object" is what you can get physically. You see this person primarily as a body. You are not that interested in who he is emotionally or spiritually.

- **Infatuation is mental desire.** It is full of emotion and intrigue. You are obsessed with your "love object." Her image captivates you. You want to know more. This infatuation can be physical, too. As with lust, you are mainly interested in what you can get from this person.

- **Love is spiritual desire.** Love is full of desire. You are intent on knowing the whole person and not just his image. Images that "fall in love," and even marry each other, are still strangers. Love beckons us to drop the mask and to stop hiding. Then the real dance can begin. In love, the real desire is not about what I want *from you;* it's about what I want *for you.*

With unconditional love, you care about each other's well-being. You are each other's friend. This is true whatever the form of your relationship is. Friendship is the heart of love. Parents and children learn to love one another by growing a friendship that is beyond roles. Romance without friendship does not last, but romance between friends renews itself forever. Unconditional love expresses itself between friends who tell each other, "I want the best for you." Crucially, friends do not say, "I want for you what I want for you." What they say is "I want for you what you want for you." Unconditional love is full of kindness and generosity like this. Kindness is everywhere in love, and, above all, there is no harm or meanness.

> *"To love is . . . to will the good of another."*
>
> **Thomas Aquinas**

Here's how you really know if you love someone and if someone loves you: *you both want each other to be happy.* Each other's happiness means more to you than anything else. Happiness is sacred because it is an attribute of love, and when you are happy it helps you to love each other more. If I know that you are truly happy, and that I am happy too, it is a sure sign we are in the flow of love. It is also a sign that we are being true to each other and ourselves. We would never stand in the way of one another's happiness, even if that meant being apart, because most of all we want the people we love to be who they truly are, to follow their hearts, and to live the lives they are called to live.

Chapter 11

I Love You

In the Loveability program, I teach a series of inquiries on the meaning of love. These inquiries may look plain and simple on paper, but when you give yourself over to them, you discover they are luminous and rich with insight. Like all good inquiries, they are a kind of philosopher's stone that imparts more clarity and healing each time you hold them in your mind. These inquiries are so enlightening that they can transform your relationship to love and, thereby, enable you to experience more joy and less pain in all your relationships. One example of these inquiries is the I Love You Inquiry.

The I Love You Inquiry can be done in small groups (as in the Loveability program) or in pairs (especially good for couples and with family members), and also on your own. This inquiry has three parts. In Part One, you complete the following sentence ten times: *When I say "I love you" I mean . . .* I recommend you get a pen and paper and do this now before reading on. If you don't have a pen, do it out loud or in your mind. Notice any responses that arise in you. Be aware of sensations in your body, feelings in

> *"I know no ways to mince it in love, but directly to say 'I love you.'"*
>
> **William Shakespeare**

your heart, and thoughts in your mind. Listen to yourself, be curious, and allow yourself to go with the flow.

How did you get on? A lot of my students report some difficulty doing this inquiry. In one Loveability course, a lawyer named Daniel told the group, "I must have said 'I love you' to my wife at least ten thousand times, but this is the first time I've consciously thought about what it means." A doctor named Helen said, "When I say 'I love you' to my children I really mean it, but I'm not exactly sure what it means." To add to the confusion, students often report that saying "I love you" can mean something different each time they say it. "It depends who I say it to" is another common response I hear.

The meaning of "I love you" has been tainted for some. For example, Claire, a nurse, who attended my first Loveability program, told the group, "I find it difficult to know what 'I love you' means because I was raised in a family in which I never heard those words spoken." Janice, a schoolteacher, said, "My parents made me say 'I love you' to them every night before bedtime, even when I didn't want to. I guess I still have some healing to do on these words." Many students have told me that although their parents said "I love you," they didn't feel loved by them. The meaning of "I love you" was distorted by their parents' behavior that was manipulative, possessive, critical, or controlling.

Those three simple words—*I love you*—can cause a lot of confusion and pain in romance, too. "My first serious boyfriend left me after I told him 'I love you,'" said Paula. "I ended an engagement to my fiancé because he couldn't say 'I love you,'" said Katrina. "My last boyfriend said 'I love you' only when he wanted sex," said Julie. "When my girlfriend says 'I love you' I feel a pressure to say it back to her," said Kevin. "Each time my ex-husband was physically violent to me, he'd apologize and say 'I love you' in the sweetest way," said Carole. "The only girl I've ever said 'I love you' to betrayed me with my best friend," said James.

In Part Two of the I Love You Inquiry, you complete the following sentence five times: *When I say "I love you" what I really mean is . . .* The aim here is to help you be more conscious and clear about what you mean when you say "I love you." Upon reflection, many students notice that the meaning of "I love you" has changed for them as they have grown and matured. Michelle, who contributed to an I Love You Inquiry I hosted on Facebook, wrote, "Looking back through the years I realize I used to say it and hope it was said back to me to prove I was loveable. Thankfully these days I know I am loveable, and I say it so as to verbally express the fullness of my feeling for my daughter, my friends, and my family and all that exists."[1]

In Part Three, you reflect on what was the most truthful thing you said or heard in your I Love You Inquiry. Here are a few of my reflections:

- In truth, the words *I love you* are an affirmation that love is present; love is what brought us together; and in love we are joined.

- The real meaning of *I love you* is not found in the words themselves, but in the intention behind them.

- When I speak the words *I love you* I often feel as if love itself has made me speak out. "Therefore, when I say that 'I love,' it is not I who love, but in reality Love who acts through me," wrote Robert A. Johnson in *WE: Understanding the Psychology of Human Love.*[2]

- Most of all, "I love you" has no meaning or value until it can be said unconditionally to one and without exclusion to all.

"I See You"

One of the most persistent myths about love is that *love is blind*. Only the blind could say such a thing. Not loving is the cause of blindness. When someone says to you "I love you," and says it from the heart, it is because

> "Love is born from both the eyes and the heart."
>
> **Joseph Campbell**

he or she is a witness to the essence of who you are. In simple translation, "I love you" means "I see you." Love has turned this person into a seer. Unlike love's impostors, infatuation and lust, which offer only a partial perception, love sees with the heart and it sees the whole person. Love sees your eternal loveliness. Love sees how loveable you really are.

When people say to you, "I love you," and it is meant truly, they are not relating to you as just a body; they see your soul. Love is not blind; it is visionary. Love sees past physical appearances. Someone who loves you sees that you *have a body*, but doesn't think you *are a body*. How you look is not who you are. Similarly, someone who loves you recognizes you are a good person, a kind person, and a loving person, for example, but sees beyond that too. This person recognizes that you have a personality, but knows you are not just an image or a set of behaviors. Love sees something more. In essence, *love is what you experience when your soul sees the soul of another.*

I first encountered the idea that love is souls seeing one another when my friend Avanti gave me a copy of *The Upanishads*. An Upanishad is a Hindu psalm or gospel that explores the nature of reality. Here, "reality" means *that which exists beyond physical appearances.* One of the earliest Upanishads is the Brihadaranyaka Upanishad, written in the 9th century B.C. I remember typing out a few stanzas from this Upanishad on my old Imperial typewriter. I have meditated on them many times since and have also read them out at several weddings. Here they are:

> **not for love of the husband is a husband dear,**
> **but for love of the Soul a husband is dear;**

> **not for love of the wife is a wife dear,**
> **but for love of the Soul a wife is dear;**

> **not for love of the sons are sons dear,**
> **but for love of the Soul sons are dear;**

**not for love of the beings are beings dear,
but for love of the Soul beings are dear;**

**not for love of the gods are the gods dear,
but for love of the Soul the gods are dear;**

**not for love of all is all dear,
but for love of the Soul all is dear.**[3]

Love leads us from the unreal to the real, *and* it reveals an even greater mystery. The mystery is that everyone we truly meet and see is somehow already familiar to us. "I love you" doesn't just mean "I see you"; it also means "I recognize you." This recognition can happen in less than five seconds of the first meeting or it may happen gradually over time.[4] When you love someone, you want to know everything about them, and yet you feel as if you know them already. In love, you meet each other. However, it's not like two brand-new people are getting to know each other for the first time; rather, it feels more like two old acquaintances—timeless friends—experiencing a blissful reunion.

Isn't this so? Each time I make a new friend, I am struck by how familiar this person feels to me. As a four-year-old boy, I remember looking at my brother, David, who had just been born, and thinking, *My friend is here at last.* Where on earth did that thought come from? Truly, there is always more to love than meets the eye. The first time I saw my children, Bo and Christopher, I felt like I'd known them forever. And I will never forget how, on my first date with my wife, Hollie, what I felt wasn't so much "I love you" as "I love you already."

I wrote a poem for Hollie early in our romance in which I tried to express this feeling of "I love you already." The poem was called "Pages of My History." Part of it reads:

**By some grace, we are back together,
as if we'd never been apart.**

**Somehow you are present in the
pages of my history now.**

**I can see you in people and places,
and in times gone by.**

**We have always been together,
always and everywhere.**

In love, there is even another level of seeing. "I love you" is like a greeting that honors our essential relatedness. It is a recognition that when any two of us meet, there is only one of us here. In love, we experience what Martin Buber describes in his book *I and Thou* as a "wholeness of being" in each other and a "unity of being" between each other. We no longer treat each other as separate objects (I-It), but rather, we see each other as expressions of the same love (I-Thou) that is both divine and universal. "All real living is meeting," wrote Buber.[5] Love helps us to see each other. Love also gives us the courage to be seen. In love, we bring each other fully into existence.[6]

> *"Lovers don't finally meet somewhere. They're in each other all along."*
>
> **Rumi**

There is only one question you need to consider in love, which is *how many times can you fall in love with someone for the first time?* When any two people meet each other in the hidden ground of love (which Thomas Merton wrote about), they feel safe enough to reveal more of their true selves to each other. This is why in love there is always more to see. Love encourages us to keep looking, again and again, until we can see what love sees. Love is the seer. Love is the miracle that helps us to meet each other and to heal and grow together.

*"Love at first sight is easy to understand. It's when
two people have been looking at each other
for years that it becomes a miracle."*

Sam Levenson[7]

"I Accept You"

In love, we see each other because we do not judge each other. "I love you" means "I see you" and also "I accept you." To accept another person is a fully sacred act and never a half-hearted love. It means I offer you love, and nothing that is not love. Seen in this light, "I love you" is a vow of acceptance between two friends who are declaring to each other, "I will not judge you" and "I will not label you" and "I will not attack you" and "I will not condemn you." Each time you say "I love you," you are renewing this vow of acceptance and making a commitment to being the presence of love in someone's life.

The idea that love is a nonjudgmental attitude and an unconditional acceptance of another person is a central tenet of the work of Carl Rogers. I studied Carl Rogers's work in an Advanced Counseling program I took at Sandwell College when I was in my mid-20s. Carl Rogers advocated "unconditional positive regard" as an essential attitude to cultivate for a counselor, a parent, a spouse, or a friend who wants to experience genuine empathy, understanding, and growth in a relationship.[8] This unconditional positive regard is given to others *in the present* and for who they are now; it is not a reward that is saved for after they have fulfilled some imagined potential.

My lecturer, Richard Nelson-Jones, described unconditional positive regard as "an attitude of love," although it must be noted that Carl Rogers rarely used the word *love* in his lectures or writings. Another of my favorite descriptions of unconditional positive regard is by David G. Myers in the textbook *Psychology: Eighth Edition in Modules*. He writes that it is "an attitude of grace, an attitude that values us even knowing our failings."[9] Carl Rogers himself described unconditional positive regard as that which "best helps someone to be a fully functioning person."[10]

Those three words—*unconditional positive regard*—became a meditation for me. *What is it like to love someone with total unconditional acceptance?* I confess that in my first inquiry I drew a blank. My answer was *I don't know.* I could barely even imagine this, never mind practice it as a congruent counselor and friend. I saw that my mind was full of opinions, theories, stories, commentaries, and verdicts about my mum, my dad, my brother, best friends, ex-girlfriends, people I'd never met, and everyone else. Every thought I had about anyone was a judgment of one sort or another. Some judgments were friendlier than others, but still they were judgments.

My starting point with practicing *unconditional acceptance* was to accept that my mind appeared to be full of judgments about everyone I had ever loved. My first aim, therefore, was not to have "no judgments," but rather to change my relationship to these judgments. In my early inquiries I sat still, visualized someone I knew (it didn't matter who), and then watched as each judgment appeared in my mind. Instead of relating to a judgment as a gospel truth, I investigated it and I asked myself questions like:

Can I be sure this judgment is right? How do I know? Do I have the whole picture? After all, judgments are only ideas; nothing more.

What if this judgment is just a projection? Maybe I'm reading something into this situation that isn't there. Who can give me a second opinion?

What would I see if I let go of this judgment? How would I be? What would I experience? What would I do differently?

How would love see this situation? When I look through the eyes of love and don't judge anything, what do I notice?

What would it be like to have no judgments? My fear of *not judging* was that I'd become a victim of naïveté; but, in truth, what I experienced was greater clarity. Over time, I learned that when you judge a situation or a person, all you see is your judgments, but when you bring an attitude of love you see something more. I still had judgments, but I didn't believe them like I used to. Now I was more interested in seeing what I could see if I loved people instead of judging them. Gradually, I learned to trust that love has its own intelligence and its own way of seeing. I could ask love to help me see what is *real or not, true or not, kind or not, helpful or not,* and so on.

At first, I thought the whole point of *unconditional acceptance* was that I was giving someone a gift, but I quickly realized that I received a gift, too. For example, I noticed that as I judged less, I become more present, more open, and more receptive. Also, the more I gave people the space to be themselves, the more they shared who they were with me. Everyone still had an ego and occasionally put their worst foot forward, but without my judgments I could see through all this. The less I judged, the more connected I felt to everyone. A natural sense of affinity and appreciation took the place of old judgments. I discovered a happy intimacy in which, more than ever before, I could see myself in others, and I could see others in me.

Another of my early experiments in unconditional acceptance was to pay attention to what it felt like to love someone without a "because." You can try this for yourself. Think of someone you love, and find ten different ways to complete this sentence: *I love you because . . .* Notice how good it feels to do this. Next, think of the same person and simply affirm, "I love you," with no "because." Do this ten times. How does this feel? For me, it feels even better. It feels more expansive, because my love isn't limited to a list of reasons. It also feels more real (and everlasting), because my love doesn't need a "because" in order to exist. I believe there is no "because" in true love because there are no conditions in true love.

> *"Love isn't love until it's unconditional."*
>
> **Marianne Williamson**

> *"Do not seek the because—in love there is no because, no reason, no explanation, no solutions."*
>
> **Anaïs Nin**

Some say that unconditional love is a myth. They say it is impossible to love and accept others without conditions and without a "because." I agree that personalities don't know how to love, but we are more than just a persona or a mask. When we are willing to take off our mask, we discover we can love far more than we previously imagined. I believe unconditional love of others is possible if we are also willing to practice unconditional love for ourselves. In the end, it's all the same love. Unconditional love gives us the awareness (I see you) and acceptance (I accept you) that we are all equally loveable because we are made of one love.

"I Thank You"

A few weeks after Hollie and I had started dating, I woke up one morning with this burning thought on my mind: *How can I tell Hollie how much I love her and how much she means to me?* The purpose of my life that day was to find a way to tell Hollie "I love you." I had plenty of ideas, of course, like flowers, a meal, a gift, a weekend away, some perfume, but none of these expressed adequately what I really wanted to say. Eventually, I created a compilation of songs on a CD. All the songs had the same essential message. The songs included "Thank You Girl" by the Beatles, "Thank You #19" by Huey Lewis and the News, "Thank You Love" by Stevie Wonder, and "Thank You" by Alanis Morissette.

Everyone I have loved—my parents, my brother, my friends, my ex-partners, my wife, my children, my mentors—has evoked in me the same heartfelt response, and that is gratefulness. When I say "I love you" to someone, what I mean is "Thank you." To love someone is to have a deep appreciation for who they are. "I love you" means "Thank you for existing." It says, "I feel lucky and blessed to know you." "I love you" means "Thank you for being who you are." And "I feel better about the world now that I know you are in it." Love expresses itself as gratitude, and as we keep expressing our gratitude, love keeps expanding.

Love is a grateful heart. When you say "I love you" to someone, you are saying, "I am grateful for you" and "I am grateful to you." This gratitude is recognition for all this person gives to you by his or her presence in your life. You are saying, "Thank you for loving me," and "Thank you for seeing me," and "Thank you for accepting me," and, as the old lyric goes, "Thank you for letting me be myself."[11] Gratitude recognizes that none of us can discover who we really are by ourselves. It is by our undivided relatedness

> *"Your soul expresses Itself as infinite love and gratitude."*
>
> **Darren Weissman**

with each other that we experience our loveability.

If someone is in your life it is because they have a gift for you and you have a gift for them. "I love you" is a spontaneous song we sing when we want to tell someone, "Your presence is a gift in my life." "I love you" means "Thank you for helping me to love and be loved" and "Thank you for helping me to heal" and "Thank you for helping me to grow." The people we love are our friends, our teachers, and our healers. They are the essential life support we need for our journey. In *A Course in Miracles* it is stated, "It is impossible to overestimate your brother's value."[12]

> *"Only appreciation is an appropriate response to your brother,
> Gratitude is due him for both his loving thoughts and his appeals for help,
> for both are capable of bringing love into your awareness if you perceive them truly."*
>
> *A Course in Miracles*[13]

The gratitude that is expressed by true love is always deeply affirming of another person. It tells them, "You are loved for who you are." It reminds them, "You are deeply loveable as you are." It affirms their eternal loveliness. Crucially, there is no shadow in this loving gratitude. There is no "if-love," as Bernie Siegel, author of *Love, Medicine and Miracles,* put it.[14] In other words, you are not saying, "I will love you if . . ." Nor are you saying, "I will love you when . . ." In true love, there are no conditions. That is why the people you love do not have to change, to be different, or to become some-one they are not in order to earn your love and gratitude.

"I Am Here for You"

I once had the pleasure of attending a public lecture on love given by the Vietnamese Buddhist Thích Nhất Hạnh. He started his talk with a short sentence, which he referred to throughout and also repeated at the close. The sentence was: "To love is to be present." In his book *True Love,* Thích Nhất Hạnh writes, "To love, in the context of Buddhism, is above all to be there. If you are not there, how can you love?"[15] He also says, "The most precious gift you can give to one you love is your true presence."[16] Being present is the only way to recognize when love is present. It also enables you to recognize the eternal loveliness of the one you love.

Each time you say "I love you," you are really saying "I am here for you." There are many facets to "being here" for the people you love. For example:

Physically, you give your relationships the time and space they merit. "The question that arises is: do you have time to love?" asks Thích Nhất Hạnh.[17] Also, you ensure that the people you love get some of your best energy, not just the remnants.

Mentally, you give your relationships the attention they need in order to flourish. *Being here* includes setting aside thoughts of "I" so as to listen, communicate, and join fully with another person. Being present is the key to listening with love and speaking with love.

Emotionally, you are able to be present now, today, and in this moment to the person you love. Not everyone can do this. Some people are too busy to love. Others carry wounds from the past, and so they are not able to be here because they are emotionally unavailable.

Spiritually, you are happy to join with the people you love in their quest to love and know themselves better. You give your wholehearted support to their learning, growth, and healing. You show them their loveability by your actions. You love it when they follow their joy.

"I love you" is a way of saying "I am committed to you" and "I am committed to us." You are telling that person you are in this relationship. You are not waiting for the relationship to sparkle or to improve before you commit to it. You are not playing it safe. You are not wearing a mask. You are not just trying to get something. You are really here, and this relationship really matters to you. "I love you" is a statement of intent that "I am committed to loving you." And, as this is about being present, there is also another intention, which is "I am committed to being loved by you."

Sometimes "I love you" can be spoken as a blessing. For example, when we wave good-bye and shout "I love you," or when we end a conversation by saying "I love you," or when we sign a birthday card with "I love you," we are telling this person that our love goes with them. In this blessing, we convey our best wishes and we also offer love for care and protection. We recognize that life can be difficult, that there is suffering, and that this is why we are here for each other. Therefore, we offer our love to one another so that we can draw upon it for strength, guidance, and help when we most need it.

An inquiry into "I love you" really can transform our relationship to love and to each other. I will close with one final thought: *Every time you feel moved to say "I love you," it is because you recognize that "love is here."* When you tell your friend, your lover, or your child "I love you," you are acknowledging that we are always held in love—even when we can't see it. In every relationship there will be challenges and conflicts and occasions when we cannot feel the love. In these moments, one heartfelt "I love you" can restore us to love's awareness that sees that

if I am present and you are present
then love must be present, too.

Chapter 12

Show Your Love

In the summer of 1999, I walked into a bookstore in Malibu called The Malibu Shaman. The first thing I noticed was an old round wooden table with a prominent display of poetry books written by Hafiz, translated by Daniel Ladinsky. I picked up a copy of a book called *The Subject Tonight Is Love.* I held the book in both my hands, flicked it open at random to page 45, and there was a poem called "It Happens All the Time in Heaven." [1] This is how I first met one of my favorite love poems. I am grateful to Daniel for giving me the permission to publish it here:

It happens all the time in heaven,
And some day

It will begin to happen
Again on earth—

That men and women who are married,
And men and men who are
Lovers,

And women and women
Who give each other
Light,

Often will get down on their knees

And while so tenderly
Holding their lover's hand,

With tears in their eyes,
Will sincerely speak, saying,

"My dear,
How can I be more loving to you;

How can I be more
Kind?"

Hafiz and Ladinsky have given us a beautiful poem that is also a teaching and a practice. Hollie and I chose it as a reading on our wedding day. I have shared it a thousand times in counseling sessions and in lectures and workshops. In the Loveability program, I read "It Happens All the Time in Heaven" at the start of a module called "Show Your Love." In this module we explore how to make "I love you" into a full expression so that the people we love *know* they are loved by us. They don't have to guess. They don't have to be psychic. They feel our love because of how we show it.

Many of the difficulties we experience in relationships happen not because we don't love each other, but because we fail to express our love in ways that are recognizable and meaningful to each other. Love is present, always. Our task is to communicate this love in ways that people can see it, feel it, and know it. Sociologists, psychologists, and neuroscientists, for instance, recognize that while

> *"They do not love that do not show their love."*
>
> **William Shakespeare**

love is universal, we each have different ways of perceiving and expressing love. These "love differences" are described in various models and theories as "love styles,"[2] "love types,"[3] and "love languages,"[4] for example.

In examining how these love differences arise and what can be done about it, it's important to honor the differences without making them appear insurmountable. First and foremost, love is our shared interest. We all want to love and be loved. Second, it is the nature of love, being an expression of oneness, to want to overcome these differences. And third, the power of love can heal these differences if we want it to. Therefore, while you may feel a *bit different* or even *very different* from how your partner, your sibling, or your mother-in-law perceives and expresses love, you are never *too different*.

One way different love languages arise is through cultural conditioning. For example, if you have been raised in Japan instead of America, or in Iran instead of Norway, you will almost certainly have some different ideas about what love is and how love is best expressed. Inside every culture there are different religions that portray different Gods of Love, and also different ideologies about "Thou Shalt Love" and "Thou Shalt Not Love." The art, literature, and films of each culture promote their own metaphors of love. The politics of individualism or collectivism, for example, will influence a culture's relationship to love. And the media will "sell" love in ways that reflect the modern economics and values of its culture.

Cultural perspectives on love have been explored in many studies in recent times. One study, by Anna Lindstrom and Larry Samovar, interviewed people growing up in India, Iran, Japan, Norway, and the United States. Their study is full of interesting insights such as this one:

> For the Japanese, the word "ishindenshin" describes their view of love. This word literally means to communicate from mind to mind or from spirit to spirit (Tsujimura, 1968). Yet for most Westerners love involves the willingness

to *express* in words and behavior, various feelings and attitudes which exist about the relationship (Rogers, 1961).[5]

Similar studies have identified significant cultural perspectives on love. Therefore, an African man who is dating a Chinese woman, for example, would do well to consider her cultural conditioning when it comes to love. When I was in my 20s, many of my friends were from Hindu families. I also dated an Indian woman for nearly four years. I experienced firsthand how cultural conditioning plays a significant part in friendship and romance. That said, most researchers conclude that love ultimately transcends cultural differences. Susan and Clyde Hendrick, in their summary of *Love across Cultures,* report how most studies of both *passionate love* and *companionate love* find that "we are indeed more the same than we are different."[6]

Another way different love styles arise is through different upbringings in childhood. As we learned in Chapter 8, your parents' relationship to each other was the first example of friendship and romance you witnessed. How they related to each other was your first idea of a "normal" relationship. Children don't miss much. They keep a file on most things that happen in the family home. As a child, you will have noticed the tone of your father's voice when he spoke to your mother. You will have seen how warm and tactile your mother was with your father. You will also have noted how kind they were to each other, how often they laughed together, how they handled conflict, who always washed the dishes, who made most of the decisions, and how they interacted with friends and other couples.

Growing up, your relationship with each of your parents will also have influenced how you perceive and express love. This is well documented by social researchers.[7] In the Loveability program, I encourage my students to do research on their own lives. I ask them a series of questions to help them identify their parents' love styles and to note similarities and differences in their own love style. In the sitcom *Frasier,* Niles attempts to hug his older brother, Frasier, and it all becomes a bit awkward. "A handshake is as good as a hug, as our mother used to say," says Niles, as they both back away from each other.

Your personality type (or "love type") is another significant influence on how you perceive and express love. Personality theories like Myers-Briggs (based on Carl Jung's work), Transactional Analysis (based on Sigmund Freud's work), and FIRO-B (based on the Greek theory of temperaments) are helpful in raising awareness of how different personality types express love, withhold love, receive love, and block love. I teach a program on love and personality types called "Love and the Enneagram." The Enneagram identifies nine personality types, including the Helper, the Peacemaker, the Loyalist, and the Individualist, who each relate to love in their own way.

Most personality theories recognize the Extroversion-Introversion Scale or something similar. According to this scale, your personality leans toward either extroversion or introversion. For instance, you may be 60 percent extrovert and 40 percent introvert, or 90 percent extrovert and 10 percent introvert. An extroverted mother who has an introverted son would do well to learn about their differences so that they both feel loved. Similarly, introverts and extroverts who are dating, married, or just friends need to recognize and respect their differences so that they feel loved and respected. Below are some brief scenarios gathered from my counseling practice:

> *"Without outward declarations, who can conclude an inward love?"*
>
> **John Donne**

Communication Style: Sue (an extrovert) expresses her love to her husband, Dan (an introvert), by saying "I love you," sending regular texts, and asking him about his day. Dan also tells Sue "I love you," sends texts, and asks Sue about her day, *but* he doesn't do it as much as Sue, and he rarely initiates these interactions. Sometimes Sue is afraid that she loves Dan more than he loves her. When Dan sends Sue a text that isn't a reply to one of hers, she feels loved.

Social Participation: Andy (an extrovert) has a wide circle of friends and finds it energizing to socialize in big groups. His wife, Cindy (an introvert), prefers to socialize one to one and finds it exhausting trying to be friendly in large groups. Sometimes Cindy is afraid that Andy finds her boring, because on their date nights he always wants to invite another couple, too. Cindy usually agrees because she wants Andy to be happy, but on the occasions when Andy arranges a romantic meal just for two, Cindy feels really loved.

Managing the Pace: Alice (an extrovert) often gets frustrated with her eight-year-old son, Charlie (an introvert), because she experiences him as being slow. She thinks he's too shy, and so she's created a social calendar for him. She's also afraid that unless she gives him a push-start he won't do anything. Sometimes Charlie yells, "Why are we always in such a hurry, Mum?" Alice doesn't think she's in a hurry. Her pace is normal to her. Charlie likes it best when his mum relaxes and takes some time to listen to a new song he's composed on the piano.

Togetherness and Space: When Ian (an introvert) goes out on a date with his girlfriend, Tania (an extrovert), he sometimes asks her to leave the BlackBerry at home. "That way we can be alone together," he tells her. Tania agrees because she doesn't want Ian to feel like "two's company and three's a crowd." When Ian goes fishing, Tania asks him to take his iPhone with him and to keep it switched on. "That way I can reach you if I need to," she tells him. Ian agrees because although he needs his space, he knows it's important for Tania to feel connected.

Honest and Open: Suzy (an extrovert) and Martin (also an extrovert) came to see me when they were having problems in their marriage. In one session, we focused on communication. "We talk together all the time," said Suzy, "but we don't talk about everything." Martin acknowledged that they needed to communicate in a way that allowed for deeper listening and more honesty and openness. They agreed to schedule an open space once a week (no TV, no wine, no extra company, no multitasking) to catch up with each other. They called this Real Talk time.

Love and Support: Lisa (an introvert) and David (another introvert) visited me when Lisa was halfway through her chemotherapy sessions. The stress of cancer had taken its toll. In trying to cope, Lisa and David had closed down on each other. "I know Lisa isn't sharing all her feelings with me," said David, "because she doesn't want me to worry. And I'm not sharing all my thoughts with Lisa, especially my fears, because I don't want to scare her." Over time, Lisa and David agreed to let each other in more so they could support each other and feel more loved.

Above and beyond cultural conditioning, childhood upbringing, and personality type, it is your relationship to yourself—your loveability—that is the most significant influence on how you perceive and express love. When you doubt how loveable you are, you become so focused on finding love and on being loved that you may forget to pay attention to loving others. Also, your lack of self-love makes it more difficult for people to love you. In fact, they may love you very well, but you fail to notice their love because of how you feel about yourself. The more you love yourself, the better able you are to love and be loved by everyone. In love, even the differences are loveable, because we are all loveable.

The Love Map

In the "Show Your Love" module of the Loveability program, my students draw a Love Map that features at least five significant relationships in their lives. I always recommend including mother and father as two of these relationships. Sometimes my students want to omit one or both because they are estranged or in a conflict or because the parent is deceased. I've also had a couple of students who only wanted to list pets and animals. I trust that if you do this exercise you will be honest with yourself as to who is significant in your life. A typical Love Map includes parents, siblings, your partner, your children, and a best friend.

> *"In order to love simply, it is necessary to know how to show love."*
>
> **Fyodor Dostoevsky**

Once the students have completed their Love Maps, I give them a short list of questions to consider for each relationship. Here are the questions:

- **From 0 to 10, how loving is this relationship?** First, give your perception of the current health of this relationship. Then guess what score the other person would give. Better still, ask them directly, if possible. The scale is from 0 for "Not Loving" to 5 for "Okay" to 10 for "Unconditionally Loving."

- **What ways do you express your love for this person?** Try to make a list of at least ten ways.

- **What ways do they express their love for you?** Again, make a list of at least ten ways.

- **When do you feel most loved by this person?** Notice what touches you. For example, acts of kindness, loving words, physical touch, being appreciated, quality time, communicating feelings, cooking together, being noticed, having fun together, and so on.

- **When do they feel most loved by you?** Notice, for instance, if they are auditory ("I love you" is music to their ears), kinesthetic (they enjoy hugs and physical touch), artistic (they appreciate your handmade gifts), fun-loving (they love your spontaneity), and/or spiritual (they are so happy when you take an interest in what matters to them).

- **What ways could you be kinder and more loving to each other?** Here is an invitation for you to be more conscious about how you show your love. It's also an invitation to get into a conversation if possible.

I offer my students a number of assignments in the Loveability program. One is to share the poem "It Happens All the Time in Heaven" as a prelude to a conversation about love. Another assignment is to invite a friend, partner, or relative to go through the Love Map questions together. When partners attend the Loveability program together, I give them a sentence-completion exercise to do together. The sentence is *I feel loved by you when* . . . I encourage students to write a love letter to someone they want to express their appreciation to. And I ask parents to get creative with their children and draw pictures, make collages, sing songs, and make up bedtime stories about love.

It is the nature of love to show itself. Love wants to be known, and it wants to extend itself. Our task isn't to create love, for we are not the manufacturers of love. Neither is it to invoke love, or to make love happen, for love is already here. In love, no extra special effort is required. All that love asks is that we pay attention to love. When we pay attention, love shows us how to love each other. By making way for love, we get through to each other. As we make contact with each other, our awareness of love expands. The conditions that once set us apart, and that stood between love and us, no longer exist. Only love is here. And love is here because we are here.

PART IV

Love Knows No Fear

Lucy and Cameron had enjoyed a whirlwind romance. They first met at a wedding in Paris. They were seated opposite each other at dinner at a table that was obviously the singles' table. By the time dessert and coffee were served, Lucy and Cameron were sitting together. The attraction was instant. The conversation was fabulous. The setting was perfect. Lucy found Cameron to be handsome, bright, self-assured, and strong in a comforting sort of way. "Are you really single?" she asked him. Cameron was enraptured by Lucy's beauty, her intelligence, her wit, and her aliveness. "Are you really single?" he asked her.

The next morning Cameron flew to Hong Kong on business. He was to be away for six days. His secretary managed to book a slightly earlier flight back to Heathrow so that he could race from the airport back to his apartment, take a quick shower, and head out to dinner with Lucy. Cameron arrived at the restaurant 15 minutes late, due to traffic in Piccadilly. The maître d' showed Cameron to

> *"Let's do it, let's fall in love."*
>
> **Cole Porter**

the table where Lucy was sitting. "Are you still single?" asked Cameron as he kissed Lucy on the cheek. By way of reply Lucy asked him, "Are you still single?"

Cameron and Lucy had used their time apart to get to know each other better. Cameron had fired off e-mails to several close friends. He had learned that Lucy was 36 years old, never married, with a daughter who was 8 years old. She spoke to her mother daily. She hadn't spoken to her father in years. She was an only child. She worked as a health and beauty editor at the London office of a women's fashion magazine. She owned her own apartment in Kensington.

Lucy had arranged coffee with two close girlfriends who knew a lot about Cameron, one an ex-girlfriend. Cameron was 48 years old, twice divorced, with two daughters who lived with their mother in Hong Kong. Cameron worshipped his mother, Dotty. His father had died when he was young. He had a younger brother, Alfie, whom none of his friends had met. Cameron had a job in banking that no one understood, but it apparently paid big bonuses. Lucy and Cameron both learned something else about each other: they were, indeed, both single.

Things moved fast for Lucy and Cameron. Over the next few weeks they paraded each other before their friends. They went out to dinner most nights, attended parties on the weekends, and did sleepovers at his place. Lucy soon introduced Cameron to her daughter, Katie. She prayed Katie would be okay. She needn't have worried, though, because Katie gave Cameron a full thumbs up. Cameron drove Lucy down to Kent to meet his mother, Dotty. The meeting was okay, not great. Cameron assured Lucy that Dotty would warm up. "She's protective of me," he explained.

Three months after they first met, Cameron took Lucy back to Paris, where he proposed to her. It was a dream come true for both of them. Their friends were surprised and delighted. Katie was excited because she was going to be a flower girl at last. Cameron's daughters gave their congratulations over the phone from Hong Kong. They hadn't had a chance to meet Lucy yet. Dotty sent Lucy a beautiful card with a handwritten note that said, "Look after my son's heart, for he has a heart of gold." It meant the world to Cameron that his mother had sent Lucy her blessings.

Lucy and Cameron were no longer single. Being together was so easy and natural. It all felt so right. They were a perfect fit. They both wished they'd met each other earlier in life, but at least now they were making up for lost time. So when Cameron suggested to Lucy that they scrap the big wedding for next summer, and instead elope to Bali for a quick wedding, she happily agreed. Dotty asked Cameron to reconsider, but he and Lucy were flying high. Two weeks later, Lucy, Cameron, and a small party of family and friends, but no Dotty, boarded a plane to Bali. Lucy and Cameron honeymooned for three days in Hong Kong so that Lucy could meet Cameron's daughters.

On their return to London, Lucy and Cameron settled into their new life as Mr. and Mrs. Campbell. Lucy and Katie moved into Cameron's place in Chelsea, which was a bit of a wrench, and not ideal for Katie's journey to school each morning, but they made it work. Lucy and Cameron started house hunting together, but the market was moving slowly. In the meantime, Cameron gave Lucy the green light to make any changes she wanted to his old pad. Truthfully, she didn't like Cameron's place, or his taste in interior design, but she loved being Mrs. Campbell.

One night, about two months into their marriage, Cameron's brother, Alfie, phoned on the home line. Dotty had died unexpectedly in her sleep. She had had a stroke. That seemed to be the moment when everything changed between Cameron and Lucy. Cameron was overwhelmed with grief. Lucy tried to console him. Her consoling didn't work. She felt shut out. The funeral came and went. Lucy grew scared when Cameron's grief showed no signs of abating. She lashed out at Cameron, telling him to pull himself together. That made things worse. They started to argue. The relationship went into free fall.

That was six months ago, and now Lucy and Cameron had come to see me. They sat on the sofa, a few feet apart, and told me their story. They were both in a lot of pain. It was the sort of pain we all feel when we don't

> *"The course of true love never did run smooth."*
>
> **William Shakespeare**

feel loveable. They both looked tired. It was clear that they had withdrawn from each other. Both were afraid that the love between them had faded and was almost gone. Both had a list of grievances they wanted to tell me about. Both were ready to get out of the relationship as fast as possible. And yet both wanted it to be different this time, and not a repeat of their previous relationships.

When I meet a couple for counseling, I like to begin by having the couple introduce each other to me. So, in Lucy and Cameron's case, I asked Lucy to introduce Cameron, and then Cameron to introduce Lucy. I then ask the couple to face each other and to share what they find loveable in each other. Usually, I ask them to take turns in completing a sentence like *What I find loveable in you is . . .* I encourage them to maintain eye contact throughout. Usually, I ask the couple to complete ten rounds each. As you can imagine, this is not always easy, but I haven't met a couple yet who were unable to complete the exercise.

I always make sure to do this exercise early on, and especially before a couple starts to delve into their problems. When Lucy and Cameron did this exercise, they both enjoyed it, eventually. Afterward, they sat closer together on the sofa and held hands. The purpose of doing this exercise is not to be positive, to deny a problem exists, or to avoid anything. On the contrary, my aim with this exercise is to establish a loving context that enables a more honest and healing dialogue. I want my couples to remember that

> **the essence of who we are is always**
> **loveable, even if we have**
> **lost sight of this temporarily.**

What is likely to happen, if we don't remember this, is that two egos will project their basic fear of being unloveable onto each other. This is how we lose sight of each other. All we can see is an image of the person we once loved, and it's not a very loveable image. In fact, it's an image we have fashioned out of our own fears and then projected onto them. This is how we play the game of victims and villains. Until we stop projecting fears onto each other and start extending love, there will not be a healing outcome to any dialogue.

By talking about love at the beginning of a dialogue, I am trying to show my couples that *love is always present*. Every human relationship—not just romances—experiences a mix of love and fear, love and conflict, love and drama, and so on. When two people focus only on the story of what has happened, the *hidden ground of love* that supports them appears to shrink. Now they experience themselves and each other as oscillating between being "in love" or "out of love." This is an illusion. Everyone is always "in love," so to speak, because love is always here. That said, if all you focus on is the story, then you stop feeling the love, and that is what makes you afraid that love changes, love fades, and love ends.

To get to love you have to start with love. If a dialogue does not take place in the context of love, it will not have a loving outcome. However, if we start by remembering that we are both loveable, that we both want to love and be loved, and that love is the outcome we both desire, then we can both listen without defense and speak without attack. You don't get to a loving outcome by trying to be right, by making someone guilty, by looking innocent, by withdrawing from each other, by holding on to grievances, or by trying to control each other, for example. *Where you want to get to is where you have to start—it's true with love and with everything else.*

After I had helped Lucy and Cameron to set a loving context, we were able to engage successfully in a number of conversations, some of which I will share in this chapter. Lucy and Cameron's story is very much their own, but we can all relate. Every relationship experiences not just tests, but also stages. These stages are well mapped by psychologists, who sometimes refer to them as phases, seasons, and acts (as in acts of a play). In each act we encounter challenges, and part of the challenge is to open ourselves up to another aspect of love: its grace, its power, its majesty, its healing qualities.

Act One in loving relationships is usually *falling in love* (though there are some exceptions, like when a relationship begins with a fight). Most romances start this way, as well as when we meet a new friend, discover someone who inspires us, gaze at our newborn baby, or when we first looked into our parents' eyes. Act Two is *falling out of love* (or, at least, appearing to). In this act, we encounter all of love's opposites, including separation, fear, judgment, pain, and anger. This is when forgiveness makes its crucial entrance. After that, Act Three is about *being in love.* There are more acts after that too, all of which lead the hero of the story to give up his or her own ego in order to *know true love.*

♥ Chapter 13 ♥

The Mirror Principle

In the Loveability program I conduct a poll with my students at the start of a module entitled "The Mirror Principle." The poll consists of two statements that you decide are either true or false. The first statement is "It is easier to love others than it is to love yourself." The second statement is "The more you love yourself, the easier it is to love others." Interestingly, most students say both statements are true. How can this be? Surely, only one can be true and the other has to be false.

The first statement, "It is easier to love others than it is to love yourself," is one of the most common myths about love. It also reveals a basic misunderstanding about the nature of love. At the start of a loving relationship—in Act One, if you like—there is an act of grace. *You feel so happy and so blessed to have met each other that any doubts about your loveability are temporarily suspended.* As time goes by, however, and as the relationship takes form, this grace period ends and then you start to project how you feel about yourself onto that person and onto your relationship. This is what happened to Lucy and Cameron. It happens to us all.

The second statement, "The more you love yourself, the easier it is to love others," is one of the great truths about love. There is a theory that self-love is a block to loving others. People who teach this kind of thing have mistaken self-love for selfishness, vanity, narcissism, and other expressions of egotism. Real Self-love—with

> *"If I love myself*
> *I love you.*
> *If I love you*
> *I love myself."*
>
> **Rumi**

a capital S—is the great enabler that helps you to extend love to others. Self-love makes romance possible in every stage of a relationship. Self-love helps parents to love their children without going into endless sacrifice. Self-love helps friends to give and receive in equal measure. Self-love helps you to say "Yes" to people without saying "No" to yourself.

Relationships are mirrors. On first meeting each other, it appears we are two entirely separate entities who have "lucked out" and found each other. Over time, intimacy brings us closer. Eventually, we get close enough to see who we really are to each other. Love knows no separation. Nothing is separate, after all. Poets and physicists agree about that. The closer we look, the more we see ourselves reflected in each other. The loveliness we see in them is a reflection of our own loveliness, too. The fears and self-doubts they harbor are not that different from ours. We are different and the same all at once. It is because we are so similar that

we cannot love another if we do not love ourselves.

Every relationship in your life is a *reflection* of the relationship you have with yourself. We mirror each other. This isn't just a metaphor. Mirroring happens because of the nature of reality. We mirror each other because of our essential oneness and our basic shared interest, which is to love and be loved. Mirroring happens also because of the nature of perception. "We see things not as they are but as we are," said Immanuel Kant, the German philosopher. Perception is projection. Everyone we see is seen through the filter of our self-awareness. Therefore, how we see ourselves—loveable or unloveable—influences what we see in others.

When we meet each other we also meet ourselves. This is the Mirror Principle that operates in every one of our relationships. And because we always meet ourselves, we also can observe that in every relationship, and even in every interaction—at the most basic level—there are only two things really happening. Either we are

extending the basic truth
"I am loveable"
or
projecting the basic fear
"I am not loveable."

That's it. Nothing else is really happening. You are experiencing either the basic truth (I am loveable) or the basic fear (I am not loveable). Everything else is just a storyline that comes from this basic choice. When you are aware of your own loveableness, you naturally extend this love to others, and you find that love is easy and effortless. However, when you lose sight of your own loveableness, you project this fear onto others, and now love feels like an impossible game. Understanding how mirroring works is vital information for knowing how to love and be loved. It is the key to happiness and healing in all your relationships.

In my first session with Lucy and Cameron, I introduced the Mirror Principle to them. I also shared five principles of mirroring that I teach in the Loveability program. These five principles are set out below. After you read through the principles, I will share with you an exercise based on the Mirror Principle that I coached Lucy and Cameron on.

1. What you bring to a relationship is what you experience. You take your relationship with you wherever you go. It is with you in all your interactions with everyone. What you believe about yourself you project and/or extend onto your parents, siblings, friends, lover, children, and enemies, and onto strangers, too. You bring with you your desire to love and be loved. You bring your sense of fun, your openness, your sensitivity, and every other beautiful quality of your soul. You also bring with you any fears and doubts about love that you have not yet resolved.

You bring your relationship with your past into each new encounter. Any unfinished business is bound to make an appearance. For Lucy, the rejection she felt from her father led her to feel rejected by Cameron when he was lost in his grief. For Cameron, the grief he suppressed when his father died was hitting him hard now after his mother's death. Old wounds and lessons unlearned from the past will cause you to project fear, doubt, defensiveness, and cynicism in your present relationships. That said, the love that exists in a present relationship can help to heal the past. When you bring with you a willingness to heal, any relationship can be transformed.

2. When you think something is missing in a relationship, it is probably you. When a relationship meets a challenge, loses its excitement, or lacks something, it can be tempting to think the relationship is full of problems, but maybe it's just full of projections. My friend Susan Jeffers, author of *The Feel the Fear Guide to Lasting Love,* says the solution to most relationship problems is "to pick up the mirror instead of the magnifying glass."[1] The magnifying glass focuses on others, and therefore it tells you that your relationship can only get better if someone else does something about it. The mirror gives you self-awareness, which empowers you to make a difference so as to experience a happier and more loving relationship.

As the old saying goes, "If you spot it, you got it." Therefore, when you are tempted to blame someone, to lodge a complaint, or to make an accusation, the most loving thing you can do is to perform a self-check for any projections running the show. If you don't attend to these projections they will continue to cause mayhem in your relationships. When you think something is missing in a relationship, ask yourself these questions:

> *"If I want to be loved as I am, I have to be willing to love others as they are."*
>
> **Louise Hay**

What am I not being?
What am I not giving?
What am I not hearing?
What am I not saying?
What am I not doing?

3. No one can love you more than you love yourself and get away with it. When people don't love themselves, they accuse others of not loving them either. When you don't feel loveable, others easily trigger you. For example, when your father doesn't call you, it means (according to you) that he doesn't love you; when your partner works late again at the office, it means (according to you) that he's neglecting you; when your friends go on holiday without you, it means (according to you) they aren't your friends anymore; and when your brother shows up late for dinner, it means (according to you) he doesn't respect you. And so on.

If you won't love yourself, others will love you, but you'll have difficulty seeing it, feeling it, believing it, or trusting it. *The way you treat yourself is how you think others treat you, too.* Once again, a self-check for projections is vital. Before you accuse someone of rejecting you, make sure you aren't rejecting you, too. Similarly, before you complain about being neglected, pay some proper attention to yourself. And before you demand that others understand you better, be clear about what you are really asking for.

4. The more you love yourself, the more you recognize how loved you are. When you lose sight of your loveableness, you try to turn the other person into the source of your love. You look for your loveability in others, but you can't find it because you won't see it in yourself. You try to turn yourself into a loveable image so as to win from others the acceptance and approval you withhold from yourself. However, if you won't love yourself, you will always feel like others don't love you enough. To put it another way, until you love yourself, you will not see how much the people in your life love you.

The love you feel for others is a manifestation of the love you feel for yourself. It's all the same love. The love you feel inside your heart is what you feel when you love another person. It's all the same love. When you stop loving yourself, you end up blocking the flow of love to others. It's all the same love. When you withhold love from others, you feel unloveable. It's all the same love. The love in you is no different from the love in someone else. It exists in all of us, and in equal measure. It's all the same love.

> *"You will never feel loved until you love yourself."*
>
> **Arnaud Desjardins**

5. The more you love yourself, the more you are able to love others. When you identify with the basic fear "I am not loveable," it impairs your ability to love others. Worse still, it can cause you to hurt the people you love. For example:

> The less you love yourself,
> the more critical you become of others.

> The less you love yourself,
> the more you accuse others of not loving you.

> The less you love yourself,
> the harder you make it for people to love you.

> The less you love yourself,
> the more you try to control your relationships.

> The less you love yourself,
> the more you test other people's love for you.

> The less you love yourself,
> the more complaints you have about others.

> The less you love yourself,
> the more you fear committing to love.

> The less you love yourself,
> the more independent and defended you get.
>
> The less you love yourself,
> the more you try to change others.

Conversely, when you identify with the basic truth "I am love-able," you discover *the gift of self-love:* that is, *the more you love your-self, the more you are able to love others*. The more loveable you feel, the more love you bring to every relationship, the less you feel like something is missing, the more receptive you are to being loved, the less you block the flow of love, and the better you are able to love others. Crucially, when a relationship is difficult, like when your partner has an off day or when your child tells you she wants a new mummy or daddy, your self-love helps you to hold a space so that you don't react with defensiveness or attack.

Once I had shared these five mirroring principles with Lucy and Cameron, I gave them an exercise to do called "Tell me a way you make it difficult for people to love you." This exercise is wonderful for clearing relationships of unloving projections. I teach it in the Loveability program, and I share it almost always with couples I counsel. The self-awareness this exercise creates can save your relationships from so much pain and difficulty. When you free your mind of projections, you can see that, in truth, *love is never difficult; it is only the blocks to love that appear to make love difficult.*

When Lucy and Cameron did this exercise, Lucy began by saying to Cameron, "Tell me a way you make it difficult for peo-ple to love you." Cameron's first response was, "I cut myself off from people when I get sad." Cameron then said to Lucy, "Tell me a way you make it difficult for people to love you." Lucy said, "When people get sad, I blame myself, and I feel helpless." Over the next 30 minutes or so, Lucy and Cameron talked to each other in a way that opened up a whole new level of love, compassion, and friendship.

♥ Chapter 14 ♥

Love and Fear

I gave my first public talk on love in New York City, in a small room opposite Carnegie Hall, one Sunday morning in November 1998. I was 33 years old, and I decided that this talk was an opportunity to review what I had learned about love thus far. I called my talk "Love, Nausea, and the Wisdom to Know the Difference." The title was perfect, bearing in mind how nervous I was beforehand. For inspiration, I drew on my study of *A Course in Miracles*, which I had been studying daily for the past five years, and also on my mentoring from Tom Carpenter. I focused in particular on the relationship between love and fear.

A Course in Miracles teaches that there are two basic states of mind: love and fear. "What is not love is always fear, and nothing else," it says.[1] It also teaches that in any given moment you have only one choice to make, which is either to be loving or to be afraid. Love emanates from a feeling of oneness and from the mind of your Unconditioned Self; fear arises from feeling alone, and it is how the ego thinks. Love is described as being natural; fear is learned. When you choose fear, love appears to be not enough; but when you choose love, it can help you to heal every fear.

> *"Love is what we were born with. Fear is what we learned here."*
>
> **Marianne Williamson**

Your basic choice is love or fear. In all my reading, I had not come across such a simple description of the human story. Could it really be true? For years, I had been schooled to believe that the human mind is a labyrinth full of twists and turns with long, dark corridors and only an occasional window of light. I was taught that every mind is complex and unfathomable, made up of a unique range of rational and emotional states. *A Course in Miracles* denies all this. It teaches that our minds are the same, because all minds are joined, and that each of us is playing out the same drama of choosing love or fear.

If the one-basic-choice theory is true, then it must also be true that *all we are ever experiencing is the effect of having chosen love or fear.* I investigated this idea further by watching closely my choices and responses to everyday events. Here's what I noticed: whenever I felt good, love had something to do with it. I saw that, for example, self-acceptance is an expression of love. Appreciation is an attitude of love. Kindness is love in action. Forgiveness is a form of love. Altruism is love giving itself freely. I also noticed that when I chose love consciously I felt more connected to people, more open, more alive, and happier.

Conversely, whenever I felt bad, I was feeling fear. I saw, for example, that self-doubt is fear, that unworthiness is fear, that feeling "not enough" is fear, and so on. I noticed that there are many different names for fear, including anxiety, impatience, envy, jealousy, and skepticism. I found fear hiding behind shyness and overassertiveness, cynicism and competiveness, feeling stuck and trying too hard. I realized that judging people is born of fear, defenses are made of fear, hostility is an attack of fear, and blame is fear looking for a solution. And I noticed that fear arises when you stop loving, which also causes you to feel lonely, depressed, and powerless.

Only One Fear

In my inquiry into the basic choice between love and fear, I bumped into another idea that made everything even simpler. If it's true that there is only one love (with different expressions, not different types), then it could also be true that there is only one fear. Love can express itself in ten thousand ways, but it's all the same love, so maybe fear can also express itself in ten thousand ways, and it's all the same fear. Looked at this way, all love is an extension of the basic truth "I am loveable," and all fear is a projection of the basic fear "I am not loveable."

A Course in Miracles teaches that "nothing beyond yourself can make you fearful or loving, because nothing is beyond you."[2] Love and fear are both in you. More accurately, love is the mind of your real Self, and fear is the mind of your self-image or ego. The basic fear "I am not loveable" is the ego's private hell. This fear does not exist in reality; it exists only in your mind. It's only an idea, and as such it has no power. In fact, it would disappear if you didn't give it any attention. If you identify with it, however, you give it power. And the more strongly you identify with it, the more frightening this idea becomes. Believing this fear to be true can even cause a person to take his or her own life. It is the basis of all self-rejection.

The basic fear "I am not loveable" is the primary reason why a person stops loving himself or herself. Here starts the detour into fear and the descent into hell. The basic fear propagates itself by issuing a special guilt that is evidence and proof that "I am not worthy of love." This special guilt takes many forms. For example, Olivia, a 34-year-old New Yorker, is afraid she will never be married because she has a sexually transmitted disease; Barry, a 26-year-old soldier, is convinced he will never find love because no one would want to be with a man who lost his legs at war; and Daphne, a 55-year-old widow, is afraid she is too old to fall in love again.

One way out of hell is to challenge the basic fear "I am not loveable." When you are afraid, ask yourself, *Who is afraid?* Is it your Unconditioned Self or your self-image that is expressing this fear? Look closely. Notice which self is judging you, is defending itself, and is afraid of what might be. Notice which self believes the fear is true and which self does not. Notice how each fear comes from a thought of a separate "I." Keep looking. What is this fear made of? What is its substance, if any? The more you keep looking into a fear, the harder it is to find anything there. Keep on looking and you will see that, in truth, there is nothing to fear.

> *"The need to recognize fear and face it*
> *without disguise is a crucial step in*
> *the undoing of the ego."*
>
> **A Course in Miracles**[3]

Fear of Love

"The ego is afraid of everything," said Tom.

"Why is that?" I asked.

"The ego believes it is separate from everything," said Tom.

"But what about love?" I asked.

"The ego is afraid of love, too," he said.

"Why is that?"

"The ego fears that it is not loveable."

"So why do egos search for love?" I asked.

"So as to avoid love," said Tom.

Like me, my friend and mentor Tom Carpenter studies *A Course in Miracles* daily. Tom's mentoring helped me to see that the basic fear "I am not loveable" is what causes you to be afraid of everything else. Without this basic fear, there are no other fears. Feeling unloveable causes you to be afraid that you will not find love; it also causes you to be afraid when you do find love. This basic fear causes you to be afraid of aloneness, afraid of relationships and, most of all, afraid of love, which is the one thing that can save you from your private hell.

When you accept the basic truth "I am loveable," you welcome love into your life without any fear. You love others without any hesitation, and you let yourself be loved without any resistance. When you know you are loveable, you can see that love is safe, because love has no fear in it. However, when the rogue fear "I am not loveable" makes an appearance, it distorts your view of love so that love now appears to be full of fear and full of danger. In truth, however, love is not frightening; what is frightening is the fear of love.

> *"There is no fear in love."*
>
> **John 4:18**

Fear projects itself onto everything it sees.

Fear projects itself onto you. When you think the thought *I am not loveable,* you are not seeing who you really are; you are seeing a fearful image of yourself. When you believe that this fearful image is the real you, this is how you see yourself, and it is how you think love sees you too. Fear looks on what it has made and judges that you are either not enough or too much. Therefore, before you can show yourself to love, you must make yourself into something that is more interesting, more attractive, and more loveable. However, it's only when you see yourself through the eyes of love that you find there is nothing to fear.

Fear projects itself onto love. And when fear looks at love, it gives love all of its own attributes. Hence fear's philosophy of love is just a mirror full of fearful beliefs. For example, the fear that "I am not enough" is seen as "love is never enough"; the belief that "I don't deserve to be loved" becomes "love has to be deserved"; the idea that you have to sacrifice yourself for love is translated into "love asks for too much"; the pain of feeling unloveable makes it look like "love is painful"; holding on to unloveable beliefs about yourself leads you to believe "love fades" and "love changes" and "love does not last." What you are seeing is not love, it is fear projected onto love.

Fear projects itself onto your relationships. A Course in Miracles tells us, "Look at what you are afraid of. Only the anticipation will frighten you."[4] Fear is frightened of everything that might happen in a relationship. For example:

"What if I get hurt?"
"What if I am rejected?"
"What if it doesn't work?"
"What if I lose my identity?"
"What if it isn't real?"
"What if it isn't safe?"
"What if I lose my freedom?"
"What if I am betrayed?"
"What if it doesn't last?"

"The ego is certain that love is dangerous, and this is always its central teaching," says *A Course in Miracles*.[5] Why is the ego so afraid of love? This is a question I have pondered many times. First, it is important to remember that the ego is not who you are; it is just an image. The real you is not afraid of love, because the real you is made of love. That said, when you believe the basic fear "I am not loveable," everything is frightening, including love. Love is frightening because the ego cannot accept both the thought of love and its basic fear. Love and fear cannot coexist. The ego understands that *love is letting go of fear.* It understands that in love there is no ego.

Love Heals Fear

All my friends fell in love before I did. Some fell in love a lot. I didn't. I tried to make myself fall in a love a couple of times, but I just couldn't do it. My friends told me I was afraid of love. I just wanted it to be real. And so I saved myself for the real thing. When I finally did fall in love I felt fantastic, for about five days. After that, I felt terrible. I was in love and nauseous. I didn't expect that. I canceled our next date. I didn't return her calls. I needed time to think. What was wrong with me? Love should feel better than this. Eventually, I decided to tell my girlfriend the truth. "I love you, and I'm frightened," I said. Her response was "Me too."

Two weeks later, my girlfriend and I were sitting in a workshop led by Sondra Ray called "Love Is Letting Go of Fear." Sondra, a former nurse and family sociologist, is the founder of Loving Relationships Training (also known as LRT).[6] Her work is inspired by many wisdom traditions, especially from India and Hawaii. She is also a student of *A Course in Miracles*. For three days she coached 40 people on the physical, emotional, and spiritual mechanics of how to be less afraid and more loving. Everything Sondra shared with us was noteworthy. My biggest takeaway was learning about this central tenet of her work:

**love brings up everything unlike itself for
the purpose of healing.**

Love and fear have an opposite effect on you. The principal effect of fear is that it prevents you from seeing where love is present, whereas love helps you to see where you are afraid. Love makes you conscious. It switches a light on in your mind. This light brings everything into view. You can see into every corner of your mind. Love does not judge, so nothing is hidden. Love does not condemn, so there is no deception. Love does not censure, so all is revealed. Love exposes the fears you identify with, the secret shame you haven't forgiven, the old wounds not yet released, and every other unloving thought that blocks the awareness of love's presence.

"Love heals fear," said Sondra. "And love frees you from the fearful image that is your ego." In a truly loving relationship—which is your magic mirror—the other person shines love on you so that your relationship with yourself comes into full view. Love shows you what you really think of yourself and also how you relate to yourself. Love and fear cannot coexist. Therefore, you cannot be loved by someone and continue to believe "I am not loveable." Similarly, you cannot say "Yes" to love and continue to judge yourself, to reject yourself, or to negate yourself. Love raises the debate. It asks questions like

Are you loveable? Yes or No?

How willing are you to put love
first in all your relationships?

How willing are you to love another person?

And how willing are you to let yourself be loved?

How much love is possible, and how
much is too good to be true?

When someone loves and accepts you unconditionally, it brings up all your fears about love. For example, if you think that love exists outside you, you will be terrified of losing love. Or, if you believe that love has an agenda, you will protect yourself against love. Or, if you fear that love does not last, you will control things when it gets really good. Love helps you to heal your relationship to love by showing you how you make love so difficult. Love brings all your choices into full view. You have to choose between love and fear, love and cynicism, love and defensiveness, and love and the ego.

What I learned from Sondra is that love is the best attitude for facing your fears. When afraid, the loving response is to see if the fear has any merit. For example, if you are afraid to commit romantically to someone, maybe this fear is telling you, "He/she is not right for you." Susan attended a recent Loveability program. She is 25 years old, and she is engaged to Dan, a 38-year-old heroin addict, who refuses to get help. She told me, "I'm afraid that if we get married it won't last." Sometimes fear has a point. Once Susan stopped judging the fear, she began to get clear about what she was really afraid of. As she met each fear with love, she also got clearer about what to do next.

Love's awareness helps you to look into a fear to see if anything is really there. You cannot get to the truth if you avoid a fear, or judge a fear, or are afraid of a fear. Love brings fear into full view so that you can see if there is a message for you, a lesson for you, or even a gift for you. This is how love heals fear. This is how love helps you to be fully present, undefended, and open to your life. *Love brings up everything unlike itself so that you can let go of fear and be the loving person you truly are.*

Chapter 15

Love Does Not Hurt

"It was the first time I was ever in love, and I learned a lot. Before that I'd never even thought about killing myself."

Steven Wright, comedian

"If you could teach your children only one lesson about love, what would it be?" I was asked this question in a recent interview I gave on the radio. It's a great question. It really made me think. How would you answer it? There are many answers I could have given, but I was asked to give just one. What came to my mind was a mantra I learned from my great friend, psychologist Chuck Spezzano. I teach about this mantra in every Loveability program. The mantra is: *If it hurts, it isn't love.*

I first came across Chuck Spezzano's work in the summer of 1998. A friend of mine gave me a book that Chuck had self-published. It was called *If It Hurts, It Isn't Love.*[1] The title got my attention. The book consists of 366 daily meditations on the psychology and spirituality of love. I was so inspired by what I read that I contacted Chuck and arranged for his book to be published by my publisher at the time. I wrote the foreword to the new edition and helped to promote the book through my work. I have read *If It Hurts, It Isn't Love* many times, and it is one of my favorite books on love.

Like most people, I had experienced a mix of joy and pain in my relationships. The most pain I experienced was always with the people I loved the most. The metaphor that describes love as a beautiful flower with thorns seemed accurate enough to me. I believed that love is the greatest happiness and also that love hurts. I didn't question the idea that love hurts until I read Chuck's work and attended several of his excellent seminars, some of which he co-presented with his wife, Lency Spezzano,[2] through their organization called Psychology of Vision.[3]

Chuck's work encouraged me to reexamine my ideas about the relationship between love and pain. What I learned is that when you look more closely at love and pain, you realize that *love and pain are not the same thing.* Love is always love. It is only ever love *and nothing else.* There are no additives or poisons in love. Therefore, the effect of love can only ever be love. This makes sense, doesn't it? If love is only made of love, it is surely not possible for love to hurt you or cause you any harm. The question then remains, if it isn't love that hurts us, what is it?

"Pain is just an unlearned lesson," says Chuck Spezzano. "It's your mind's way of saying that you have made a mistake."[4] One theory, then, is *it's not love that hurts, it's the mistakes we make in love that cause us hurt.* For example, the pain of betrayal is caused not by love but by deceit; the pain of loss is caused not by love but by our attachment to a form; and the pain of conflict is caused not by love but by some unmet need, perhaps. What hurts is not love itself, but rather our unloving actions and reactions, the conditions we place on love, the fear that we are not loved, our resistance to being loved, and even our lack of faith in love.

You experience pain when you are thinking, feeling, or behaving in a way that is *not loving.* When you bring a loving awareness to this pain, you can see what is really hurting you. In the Loveability program I share a teaching aid with my students called the True Love Checklist, which identifies ten common mistakes about

> *"Love cannot create hurt; it is the healer of hurt."*
>
> **Mike George**

love that can cause hurt and pain in relationships. The True Love Checklist is designed to help you be aware of any mistakes you are making, recognize the real cause of pain, learn any unlearned lessons, and, most of all, choose a better way.

True Love Checklist

1. Is this love or fear? The basic fear "I am not loveable" is the primary cause of all suffering. When you identify with this fear, it causes many tears to fall. The fear is not true, but if you believe it, you will turn away from yourself. Feeling unloveable causes you to reject your eternal loveliness. Instead, you put on an act that takes the place of your true self in the hope that this will trick people into loving you. However, because you have rejected yourself, you are afraid that everyone else will reject you, too, especially when they get to know the truth about you.

When you believe "I am not loveable," it causes you to contract inside, to defend yourself, and to behave in unloving ways that add to your pain. You also experience pain when fear appears to triumph over love: for example, when it looks like love is not present, that love changes, that love is being withheld, that love is not enough, and that love dies. In deep pain, the fear is that love has forsaken you. In other words, love

> *"The cause of your suffering is you do not love enough."*
>
> **Caroline Myss**

has rejected you, too. This is your private hell. The temptation here is to reject love. However, when you stop loving, it hurts you even more. Only by loving can you begin to face the fear, heal the pain, and walk out of hell.

2. Is this love or dependency? Many psychologists view dependency as a major source of pain in love. They counsel you against needing anything from anyone, lest you get hurt. One way to counteract this fear of dependency is to be totally independent of others. Unfortunately, this causes just as much pain. Independence looks like freedom, but really it is a dead end. It shuts you off from the whole of creation. Imagine if you had no relationships in your life. I grant that this might appeal to you sometimes, but for most it is only a passing thought. The truth is, we depend on relationships for our growth and evolution. Relationships are how we learn to love and be loved.

Healthy dependency allows you to ask for help, to be open to inspiration, to cooperate with others, and not to try to do life by yourself. Unhealthy dependency arises when you feel unloveable and see others as the source of your love. This causes you to enroll your mother, your partner, or your children, for instance, into making you feel more loveable. They may not know it, but they have a contract of employment. You believe it's their job to make you feel whole, secure, and connected to the world, to heal your wounds, and to validate you. Inevitably, though, when you make someone your source of love, they will also be a source of pain. No one does a very good job making someone feel loveable, mostly because it's an impossible task.

People can encourage you to feel loveable, but they can't make you feel loveable. Making sure you feel loveable is your job, not someone else's.

3. Is this love or attachment? Can you feel the difference between feeling connected with and feeling attached to someone? When you love someone, you feel a connection that defies all physical laws. You feel connected from the moment you first recognize each other. Your friendship is timeless. You feel connected even if you live ten thousand miles apart. Your friendship knows no distance. You feel connected even if you haven't spoken in ages. Your friendship is beyond words. You feel connected even if one of you is in heaven and the other is still here on earth. Your friendship is beyond all form. Your love for each other serves as a memory of your true nature, and somehow you know that your connection will continue long after you have forgotten about your visit to this world.

When you are attached to someone, it is still possible to feel the love that connects you, but mostly what you feel is fear, anxiety, and pain. Attachments are contracts based on form. Pain arises when the conditions of attachment are not met. For example, "I do, hereby, expect you, lawfully, to agree not to change too much, or grow too much, or become so happy that you don't need me. The penalty for such unlawful behavior is shame." Pain also arises when the form of the relationship changes. Children grow up and leave home. Parents divorce and leave home. Our best friend gets married. Our father gets married again. We get married and divorced. People we love die. We grieve the loss of form, and understandably so. But, in truth, there is no loss in love, not when you allow yourself to feel your genuine connection to each other.

4. Is this love or do I have an agenda? What do you expect from your mother? What do you expect from your lover? What do you expect from your child? What do you expect from the world? Whenever your expectations are not met, you will know it, because you will feel disappointed, let down, angry, and hurt. What is the difference between an expectation and a demand? Nothing much, actually. Expectations look innocent enough, but they carry an agenda, a plan, and a demand to get something. Each expectation is set on a timer, and if you don't get what you want in time, the bomb goes off.

Expectations are fear based. They are an effort to grab what you want instead of letting it come to you. The more afraid you are of not getting what you want, the more expectations you have on your list. Expectations are frustrating because they arise from an attitude of getting that blocks receptivity. They create an agenda that acts like a wall between you and the other person. Love doesn't have an agenda, because an attitude of love is really based on *being* rather than on *getting* and *receiving*. In other words, love helps you to *be* what you want to give and receive.

Here is a list of common expectations that cause hurt in relationships. As you take each expectation off your list, it frees you up to love and be loved.

- I expect to be loved by everybody.

- I expect people I love to love me, too.

- I expect people I love to love me more than others.

- I expect others to know how I need to be loved.

- I expect others to love me the way I love them.

- I expect people I love to know that I love them.

- I expect others to love me without an agenda.

- I expect others to love me without making mistakes.

- I expect others to love me all the time.

5. Is this love or am I trying to get something? "You can't feel hurt unless you are giving to take," says Chuck Spezzano.[5] Imagine you are walking down the street. A stranger approaches. You smile and say, "Hello." The stranger doesn't respond. How do you feel about that? Do you feel foolish for having said "Hello"? Do you feel rejected? Are you offended that they ignored you? If you feel any hurt at all, the chances are it's because you wanted that person to give you something. Your "Hello" wasn't just a greeting; it was a trade. What did you want? Was it attention? Was it connection? Was it love?

When you give love in order to get love, it ends in tears, either right away or eventually. Love is not something to get. You can't get love from people like you get a bottle of soda from a vending machine. If you did a naked dance in front of them, you could probably get their attention, some approval, and even wild applause. This might feel pretty good, but it wouldn't be love. If you give love in order to get love, you will end up feeling disappointed and

> *"Personalities don't love, they want something."*
>
> **Byron Katie**

resentful. "Look what I did for you," you yell. "I even did a naked dance for you," you cry. When you give love freely, you feel the love you give and you feel loveable no matter what the return.

6. Is this love or am I in sacrifice? There are two types of sacrifice: *unhealthy sacrifice* and *healthy sacrifice*. One is based on fear and the other on love. Knowing the difference is a key to knowing how to love and be loved.

Over the years, I have counseled people who tried to use *unhealthy sacrifice* to save a marriage. It appeared to work at first, but love and dishonesty are not good bedfellows. I have seen lovers try to play small in a relationship so as to heal power struggles and avoid rejection. I have seen children get ill in a desperate attempt to heal their parents' relationship. I have seen business leaders nearly kill themselves for their cause. Unhealthy sacrifice is often well intentioned, but it doesn't work, because it is based on fear and not love.

Healthy sacrifice is a different story. To be happy in a relationship, you have to be willing to sacrifice fear for love, independence for intimacy, resentment for forgiveness, and old wounds for new beginnings, for instance. Above all, you have to stop giving yourself away and learn how to give more of yourself. You give yourself away when you are not true to yourself, when you play a role, when you don't speak up, when you don't ask for what you want, when you don't listen to yourself, and when you don't allow yourself to receive. *The key is to remember that whatever you are trying to achieve with unhealthy sacrifice can also be achieved without it.*

7. Is this love or am I in a role? Two people in a loving relationship will play out any number of roles together. These roles are interchangeable, spontaneous, and worn lightly when both people are happy and all is well. Indeed, you barely notice that these roles exist. However, when things are not okay, the roles are more fixed and rigid. They are your position and your point of view in the relationship. They affect your capacity to give and to receive. They can cause you to polarize and to oppose each other. This is painful, as you no longer feel like you are on the same team. This perceived separation can cause power struggles and more conflict.

Roles that are fixed and rigid cause hurt and pain in relationships. These roles usually begin in childhood, born of a fear that you are not loveable or that there is not enough love to go around. Role-playing is a strategy—your ego's best effort—for winning love and avoiding pain. Unfortunately, taking on a role is *a strategy to get love that prevents you from being able to give and receive love.* When there is a problem in a relationship, your homework is to find out what role you are playing, and also to consider what good things could happen if you stopped playing this role. Here are some examples of roles that cause polarity and conflict:

**Am I loving this person or am I playing
the role of the provider or the martyr?**

**Am I loving this person or am I playing the independent role
or the dependent role?**

**Am I loving this person or am I playing
the role of the parent or the child?**

**Am I loving this person or am I playing
the role of the rescuer or the victim?**

**Am I loving this person or am I trying
to be positive or being contrary?**

8. Is this love or am I trying to change the person I love? Have you tried to change your partner recently? How did you get on? Were they suitably appreciative? I imagine you didn't get a thank-you note for your efforts. Have you tried to change your children? Were they receptive? Did it work this time? Children are willing learners, except when they don't feel loved. Have you tried to change your parents again? After all, they're getting older now and so they should be weaker and less able to resist your campaign. Has anyone tried to change you recently? How did you feel about that? Did you feel more loved? Are you feeling even more love for that person who wants to change you?

A common mistake in relationships is the belief that your love will change a person, eventually. *You can't love someone and want him or her to change.* For a start, when you try to change people, they do not feel loved by you. If anything, they feel judged and rejected. Love does not seek to change people, because love does not find any fault in a person's true essence. Love can help a person to grow and to bring out the best in him or her; but you will not see any of this if you do not love the person unconditionally in the first place. The paradox of love is that *when you stop wanting each other to change, you are changed, and this change enables you to love each other more.*

Ask yourself these questions:

- Am I loving this person or am I trying to fix him?

- Am I loving this person or am I trying to improve her?

- Am I loving this person or am I trying to save him?

- Am I loving this person or am I trying to heal her?

- Am I loving this person or am I trying to get him enlightened?

9. Is this love or am I trying to control this person? The joke goes, "When a man and woman marry, they become one. The trouble starts when they try to decide which one." Every relationship experiences what is commonly called a power struggle. This is true not just in marriage, but also in relationships between parents and children, between in-laws, and between siblings, for instance. In a power struggle, both people have to learn to give up trying to control each other so as to experience true friendship and love. When a power struggle is healed, it helps both people feel more equal, more connected, and more loved.

Control is a form of fear. When you are tempted to control the relationship, it's because you're afraid that you are unloveable and that you might lose someone's love. Unfortunately, the more you try to control a relationship, the less loving it feels. If only one of you is authorized to take the lead, make the decisions, and drive the car, so to speak, you run into problems. Too much control makes the other person passive or passive-aggressive. The more you control someone, the less attractive and interesting the person is to you. Controlling the relationship makes it less exciting and less fun. Control stunts growth. It kills the aliveness. The relationship is a dead fish. Here are some points to consider:

- Am I loving this person or am I playing it safe?

- Am I loving this person or am I trying to protect him?

- Am I loving this person or am I trying to protect myself?

- Am I loving this person or am I trying to keep the peace?

- Am I loving this person or am I trying to hold on to her?

10. Is this love or am I trying not to get hurt? If you believe that love hurts, you will be afraid to love and be loved. This fear of love makes you want to protect yourself against love. Your ego creates an arsenal of defenses that stop you, for instance, from loving too much or loving too easily. You employ these defenses to feel safe, in control, and emotionally insured against any injury. And still you get hurt. And hurt again. Eventually, by some act of grace, you consider the possibility that these defenses are the cause of your hurt. And so it is, because defenses are made of fear and fear keeps you stuck in the experience you are trying to escape from.

Until you realize that love doesn't hurt, love will always appear to hurt you. That will be your story, anyway. If you are willing to let go of your story, even for just a moment, you can start to have a different experience of love. When you open your mind to the possibility that *if it hurts, it isn't love,* you stop being so afraid of love. As you begin to dismantle some of your old defenses, you notice that the course of love runs

> *"One word frees us of all the weight and pain of life; that word is love."*
>
> **Sophocles**

more smoothly. Each time you let go of another defense or an old wound, for example, you experience more love. Eventually, your defenselessness opens you up to an experience of pure love.

PART V

Love Is the Answer

When my friend Andy Thrasyvoulou invited me to spend a week on retreat on Mount Athos, it felt like an answer to a prayer. I accepted right away, and with Andy's help I applied for the necessary permit from the Mount Athos Pilgrim Bureau. At the time of my visit, a maximum of 100 permits per day were issued to Orthodox Christian visitors and only 10 permits per day for non-Orthodox visitors. Happily for me, my application was accepted. With my permit in hand, I met up with Andy, his two sons, and two friends for breakfast at Heathrow. We flew to Thessaloniki, traveled by car to Ouranoupolis, and then boarded a boat to Daphne (or Dafni), the seaport of Mount Athos. We arrived at our monastery just in time for evening prayers.

I woke up early on my first morning on Mount Athos. The window in my little dormitory had no curtain to keep out the light. I got dressed, put some provisions in a backpack, and went out to explore. About 200 meters away from the monastery I found a perfect spot for my morning meditation. It was a big, soft rock on the edge of a small hillside that looked out over the Aegean Sea. Two old, leafy olive trees stood next to it. The sea looked like a lake. The cool morning air tasted sweet. The bell in the monastery started to ring. That was my cue to begin my meditation. I already felt at home on the Holy Mountain (the name Greek people give to Mount Athos).

Every morning, I visited the big, soft rock. I took with me a bottle of water, a pen, a notebook, and something to read. I'd stay there until about midday, when the sun would appear from behind the hill that the monastery was built into. Later in the day I would return to my meditation seat. The two olive trees provided just enough shelter from the hot, orange afternoon sun. Many of the meditations and inquiries I did on Mount Athos are here in this book. It was on the Holy Mountain that I first conceived the idea of Loveability.

Each evening I joined Andy and our party to watch the sun go down. Afterward, we sat in a circle and talked for a while. Up above us, the big white stars lit up the black night sky. These were precious times, and we all knew it. Occasionally, we joined the monks in the monastery for the evening meal and for evening prayers. One night, we attended a ceremony at midnight to celebrate the Transfiguration of Christ, considered by many Christians to be the highest point of Jesus's earthly life. The event is recorded in the first three Gospels (Matthew 17:1–9; Mark 9:2–9; Luke 9:28–36).[1] It takes place on a mountain where, before Peter, James, and John, Jesus's physical body dissolves into the light of divine love.

On the fourth morning of my retreat, I was sitting on the big, soft rock when I noticed I had a visitor. He was a monk from the monastery. He was about 30 years old, dressed in a long black garment, with brown sandals, a shaved head, and a handsome face.

"I have a question for you," said the monk, by way of a greeting.

"What is it?"

"Do you believe in God?" he asked.

"Yes, I do," I said.

"So you are a Christian?"

"I believe Jesus knew about God," I said.

"Good," he said.

We were friends, for now. However, his questions sounded like a test, not an inquiry. Also, I could tell he still had more questions for me.

"What church do you belong to?" he asked.

"I don't," I said.

"Then you are not a Christian," he told me.

"Why is that?"

"You have to belong to a church."

"Which church did Jesus belong to?" I asked.

"You have to belong to a church," he repeated.

The monk was obviously annoyed with me, but I wasn't sure why. I learned later that he'd taken offense to my meditating outside the monastery.

"What type of a Christian are you?" he pressed.

"I'm not a type," I said.

"You have to be a type of Christian," he said.

"What do you mean?"

"Are you Orthodox, Roman Catholic, Protestant, Anglican?"

"I am none of those," I said.

"None?" he said, looking dismayed.

"Can you forgive me for not being a type of Christian?" I asked.

The monk paced around me as I sat on the big, soft rock. He had one more round of questions for me.

"Do you believe in Jesus?"

"Yes, I do."

"Do you believe he was the only Son of God?"

"I believe Jesus was a messenger of love," I said. "And I also believe that other great spiritual teachers, like Buddha, Lao Tzu, Muhammad, and St. Francis of Assisi, came to teach us about love, too."

"But do you believe Jesus was God's only Son?" he asked again.

"Do you believe God is a man in the sky?" I asked back.

The monk walked away. He was upset. I felt sorry that we couldn't find a way to enjoy each other's company.

Later that day, in the afternoon, while I was sitting on my meditation seat next to the olive trees, I had another visitor. It was another monk. He was older than the first one. He was dressed in black, and he had a long beard that was mostly gray.

"I understand you have met Brother Leon," he said as he approached.

"I think so."

"You know, he is very angry with you," the monk said with a smile.

"Yes," I said, wondering where this conversation was going.

"I hope you can forgive him," he said.

"Of course," I said.

"He is still too full of religion to know about God."

What a great line. I smiled as soon as I heard it. Who was this monk? I had not seen him around the monastery.

"Did he ask what type of a Christian you are?"

"Yes."

"You probably aren't a type of Christian," he said with a smile.

"It's like believing there are different types of love," I said.

"One God, one Love. Is that your belief?"

"Yes."

There was a pause in our conversation for a few moments. The old monk looked out to sea.

"Do you think God is love?" I asked him after a while.

"Yes, of course," he replied.

"Me too," I said.

"Only by learning to love will we get to know God."

With that, he headed back down to the monastery. After about ten paces or so, he turned around and said something to me. The first part was in Greek, I think. I couldn't understand what he said. The next part was in English. "Only love is real," he shouted joyfully. He waved his right arm up in the air as he made his proclamation. He then continued on his way. I watched him until he was out of sight. He didn't look back. I never saw him again.

An inquiry on God has similar challenges to an inquiry on love. For instance, love is not just a word, and God is not just a name. Words are symbols; they are not the real thing. Love is not a thing; God is not a person in the sky. Neither love nor God can be defined by words, by the intellect, by the ego, by any religion, or by any science. They are indefinable because they are indivisible. They are so complete and whole that

> *"Love is the abridgement of all theology."*
>
> **St. Francis de Sales**

you can't get your head around them, so to speak. That said, it is possible to experience love and God. We can learn to recognize love, we can feel the divine, and we can allow the presence of love and God to bless us and guide us.

Over the years, I have prayed and meditated in monasteries, cathedrals, mosques, and ashrams, as well as under Bodhi trees, in stone circles, and on holy mountains. I am satisfied that what I have experienced in each of these places is the same love and the same God. Religion is love, plus politics. Sometimes there is too much politics. Religion is love, plus marketing. Sometimes there is too much marketing. In truth, you can't copyright love and you can't sell God. They are not exclusive. They don't do deals. That which created you—let's call it God—has the same attitude to all of Its creations. This holy attitude, I believe, is best described as unconditional love.

The idea that God and love are two words that describe the same experience is commonly expressed in religion and philosophy. "God is love," it is written in the Gospel of John.[2] "God is love," said Rumi.[3] "God is love," said Ramana Maharshi.[4] "God is love," states *A Course in Miracles*.[5] "God is love," sang Marvin Gaye.[6] Personally, I don't think God minds if you are into religion or not. I don't think God is that interested if you wear a cross, a star, or a crescent. However, I do think God would like you to know about love, mostly because you are an expression of love. Love is nondenominational in every way and it unites us all as one creation.

> *"When the mirror of my consciousness became clear,*
> *I saw that my family and others*
> *I love are the same as me.*
>
> *The 'you' and 'I' thought*
> *does not occur.*
> *The entire world is God."*

Lalla, 14th-century Indian mystic[7]

In the Loveability program, I teach an inquiry on love and God called "The God Meditation." Most recently, I shared this meditation with a group of 24 people who were three days away from being ordained as interfaith ministers by the One Spirit Interfaith Foundation. The God Meditation is one of my favorites. I have used it many times for my own healing and inspiration. In this meditation, psychology meets spirituality, and you get to choose between fear and love, guilt and grace, and ego and your eternal loveliness.

The God Meditation is composed of two questions and an invitation. If you did this meditation with me in the Loveability program, you'd stand with me at the front of the room. On the floor in front of us are 11 sheets of paper. The first piece of paper says "0%," the second says "10%," the third "20%," the fourth "30%," and the last says "100%." The stage is now set for the first question, which is "From 0 to 100 percent, how much does God love you?" I want your first answer, the one that popped into your head before you could think about it. I don't want a learned response. I want you to be honest with yourself.

Next, you stand on the piece of paper that matches or is closest to the score you gave, and then you reflect on how your answer affects your life. For instance, how does a score of 80 percent affect your relationship to love? Or how does 60 percent affect your relationship with others? Or how does 40 percent affect your relationship with yourself? The most common answer to this question is "100 percent." If a person's score is not 100 percent, I ask him or her to stand on the piece of paper that says 100 percent and to imagine what it's like to believe in a God that loves you and everyone else this much. Some of us are too full of fear and religion to let ourselves experience this much unconditional love.

This first question is really asking you, "Is God love?" A score of anything less than 100 percent means your answer is "No." You might tell me that God can be kind and loving sometimes, but that's not the same as saying that *God is love*. If God is loving only sometimes, it means God can also be fearful, judgmental, and vengeful, just like an ego can be. If your answer is 100 percent, you are saying that *God is love.* And this love is unconditional. That means God's love does not change, ever, and it excludes no one, not even you. In other words, this love affirms for everyone the basic truth that "I am loveable."

The God Meditation gets even more interesting when you consider the second question, which is "From 0 to 100 percent, how much do you let God love you?" Can you guess how most people answer this question? Not once has someone given me a score that is the same as or higher than the one they gave to the first question. In other words, every-one scores it lower. The last person I did this with scored 100 percent

> *"Love is not just a word. It's the knowledge of the 'I am.'"*
>
> **Nisargadatta**

for the first question and only 10 percent for the second question. She was so identified with the basic fear "I am not loveable" that she had almost (90 percent) blocked out the experience of unconditional love.

The second question is really asking you, "Are you willing to be loved?" This is the real invitation of the God Meditation. For exam-ple, if your score is currently 30 percent, I invite you to imagine what your life would be like if you increased your score to 50 percent. And after that, to 60 percent, and then 70 percent, and all the way to 100 percent. The only obstacle in your way is the basic fear "I am not loveable." That's all. One learned idea. And it's only an idea. The in-vitation is to stop identifying with that idea, if only for a day, so that you can experience what it's like to let God love you, to let life love you, to let the angels love you, and to let others love you.

Imagine living a life in which you know 100 percent that the Intelligence that created you (call it God, Source, the Universe, or whatever) loves you unconditionally and wants to support you, guide you, and inspire you. Better yet, imagine that you are 100 percent willing to let that happen. Imagine being so aligned with the basic truth "I am loveable" that you naturally extend your love to everyone, and you also let everyone love you. If you really did this, and there is no reason why you can't, you would be a mes-senger of love, too.

♥ Chapter 16 ♥

Only Love Is Real

My stay on Mount Athos gave me the space I needed to make some very personal inquiries. Each day, I sat on the big, soft rock that was my meditation seat and I thought about everything that is important. I had recently celebrated my 40th birthday. Birthdays with a zero encourage contemplation, I find. I thought about my life and my spiritual journey. I recalled lessons I'd learned from my teachers and mentors. I thought about family and friends and what they had taught me, too. I thought about my work, about the pursuit of happiness, and about what it means to live a successful life. In all my inquiries, there was one thought that was constant. It was what the old Greek monk had said: *Only love is real.*

The first time I considered the idea that *love is real* was the night my father died. My mum, David, and I left the hospital at around 9 P.M. We went back to Mum's house. We stayed up for a while. We didn't eat dinner. We weren't hungry. Death does not feel real. I couldn't comprehend how my father wasn't here anymore. Twenty years later, I still think he will walk through the door any moment now. I stayed up after Mum and David had gone to bed. I made a fire and watched the flames dance around the logs and coals. I was tired, but I didn't want to sleep.

After a while, I noticed that my mind had fixed its attention on a question. The question was *What is real?* I didn't mean to ask this question; it just appeared. *What is real?* The question wouldn't go away. *What is real?* I tried to think about something else. *What is real?* I tried not to give it any attention, but that didn't work either. *What is real?* I didn't try consciously to answer the question. *What is real?* But an answer did appear, just as the question had done. The question and the answer both formed a loop in my mind. All I did was listen.

"What is real?"
"Love is real."
"What is real?"
"Love is real."
"What is real?"
"Love is real."

I believe that this conversation was one of my father's parting gifts to me. I still feel my father's presence every day. His body doesn't exist in the form it once did, but his presence lives on, and it is as real as anything. When I think of him I remember that *love is real*.

Spiritual literature is full of the idea that love is real. Sufi poets, Christian mystics, Hindu saints, Buddhist monks, Muslim leaders, and Jewish teachers have given discourses on this. Poets like Percy Bysshe Shelley and writers like Leo Tolstoy also recognized that love is more than just a passing feeling or entertainment. The spiritual aphorism "only love is real" also appears in literature and art all over the world. In the Loveability program, I often play Carole King's song "Only Love Is Real." The lyrics are especially poignant for me. They tell the story of someone staring at a "just-lit fire" and contemplating the nature of real love.

At first glance, the idea that *only love is real* seems too big, and too abstract, to be of any use, but really it is central to the practice of love. An inquiry into *only love is real* is not a small thing, but it can help you with every little detail of your life. To do this inquiry, you are asked to let go of all your small ideas about who you are, what the world is, and what your life is really for. This can be unsettling at first, but if you stay with it, you will learn much that will help you to love and be loved. You will also experience yourself to be a far more loving person than you ever imagined you could be.

Matrix of All Matter

Fariduddin Attar was the son of an eminent scientist. He lived in the 12th and early 13th centuries. He was a scholar of Islamic literature as well as a hagiographer, which is someone who studies the lives of saints. He is also one of Iran's most famous poets, and he was an inspiration to Rumi. He wrote about many things, including consciousness and love. One of his most famous passages is this one:

> **The Eternal Wisdom made all things in Love.**
> **On Love they all depend, to Love all turn.**
> **The earth, the heavens, the sun, the moon, the stars**
> **The center of their orbit find in Love.**[1]

The mystic traditions of every faith are full of people who saw the entire universe as an intelligent system and a play of love. One of my favorite passages on this subject is by Sri Anandamayi Ma, the beautiful Indian saint from Bengal, who lived from 1896 to 1982. I am deeply grateful to yoga teacher Shiva Rea, who introduced this passage to me. It is one of the most beautiful visions of love ever written. Here it is:

> It is said that the universe has its origins in love, and the chaos is systematized into the cosmos through the bond of love.
> There is love between fire and air, between earth and water, without this love neither heaven, nor earth, nor the nether world would have originated at all. There is love between heaven and the skies, between heaven and earth,

between hell and the nether world in which it lies, and thus are three worlds supported in love.

There is love between the sun, the moon, the planets and the stars and in love they are all fixed into the sky above. There is love between the sea and its water, between the moon and the night and the sun and the day—the tree is fixed to the earth by its roots, the black bee is attached to the lotus, fish is bound to the water, man is bound to the woman—and all in love.

The body is in love with the mind and the mind with the vital prana. In love does the mother conceive the child, in love does the earth hold fast to the root of the tree, in love does the fruit accumulate juice in its kernel—thus is the whole creative process supported in love.[2]

Mystical visions of love are usually full of poetry; but they are not only poetry. Mystics like Attar and Sri Anandamayi Ma use poetry to take us beyond words, so that we can feel what is really here. Their poetry helps us to think with our hearts. It turns words into sunshine so as to convey the warmth of love. At the same time, they see love as much more than just a physical sensation, an emotion, or a positive attitude. To them, love is the Supreme Intelligence. It is the Universal Mind that holds together all of the elements in the periodic table.

Scientists used to think that the universe was made of matter. They don't anymore. "There is no matter as such," said Max Planck, the German physicist, considered by many to be the founder of quantum theory. Planck won a Nobel Prize for Physics in 1918 for his research on the nature of reality. He said, "All matter originates and exists only by virtue of a force which brings the particle of an atom to vibration and holds this most minute solar system of the atom together. We must assume behind this force the existence of a conscious and intelligent mind. This mind is the matrix of all matter."[3]

Today's science accepts that consciousness is fundamental.[4] What is this consciousness? Science doesn't have a definition for it yet. Could it be that love is the matrix of all matter? It is not beyond the realm of possibility that love and consciousness could be the same. No one can discount this for sure. In the future we will learn more about consciousness, and also more about love, and, as we do, the truth will come out. The mystics want you to know that love is consciousness with zero mass (no fear, no separation, no ego, no judgment, and no death). Centuries ago, they knew about consciousness, and also about love. It's about time we did, too.

Vital Core of Your Soul

One Sunday morning, we were all in the car on our way to visit my mum, Grandma Sally. I was driving. Bo, who was four years old at the time, was sitting next to me in the front passenger seat. Hollie and Christopher were both sitting in the back seat. To keep Bo and Christopher happy, we were listening (for the hundredth time) to *Winnie-the-Pooh,* read by Alan Bennett. Earlier that morning I had been writing an article on self-acceptance. Hollie asked me about it.

"I'm exploring the question 'Who am I without my self-image?'" I told her.

"A twist on the 'Who am I?' question," said Hollie.

"Yes," I said.

"I like it," she said.

"I guess what I'm really asking is *What are we made of?*"

"That's easy," piped up Bo.

"What's easy?"

"I know what we're made of," she said confidently.

"Okay, then, what are we made of?"

"Love and water."

Love is the one thing about you that is entirely natural. That is why love feels so good. It's also why you feel most like the real you when you choose love. Love is who you are when you stop identifying with a self-image that is

> *"Love is the vital core of the soul."*
>
> **Rumi**

trying to be good, perfect, positive, and loveable. Love is your original energy. It is the energy that animates your body and makes you feel alive. Love is the heart of who you are. It is what connects you to yourself and to others. Love is the consciousness of your Unconditioned Self. It is the intelligence you experience when you stop pretending to be neurotic.

Love reminds you who you really are. When you stop loving, you act like someone who is lost, who is a victim, and who is searching for love. This is not who you are. This is just a dream, and a fearful one at that. Your willingness to love and be loved is what wakes you up to your real, Unconditioned Self. Love offers you a total release from your self-image, your story, and your psychology. "The real nature of your being is to be loving," says Tom Carpenter. "And because your real nature is constant, that means, in truth, *there is no moment in which you do not love.*"[5]

Love is our shared identity. The differences we experience in our gender, nationality, politics, and religion do not exist in love. Once again, the mystics and the poets are clear about this. "It is love that holds everything together, and it is the everything also," says Rumi. Love is experienced when you feel at-one-ment with yourself, with another person, and with all of creation. Modern science refers to this oneness as "entanglement." Erwin Schrödinger, the Austrian physicist and winner of the 1933 Nobel Prize in Physics, referred specifically to the Upanishads when he said, "Multiplicity is only apparent; in truth, there is only one mind."[6]

Real Work of Your Life

We are a busy generation. Hopefully, the busyness is getting us somewhere. Hopefully, it's real and not just a distraction.

Since 1996, I have run a project called Success Intelligence.[7] One of our first clients was The Body Shop. "The word *love* is never mentioned in big business," said Anita Roddick, its founder.[8] We talked a lot about love at The Body Shop. Anita was passionate about helping people to follow their passion. She was a very busy person, and what she was busy about was love. Over the years, my colleagues and I have talked about love with leaders of many big brands and companies. Perhaps most notable is our work with Dove and the Campaign for Real Beauty. I was the coach to two of Dove's presidents for four years.

I describe my work with Success Intelligence as a meditation on the question "What is success?" This question is a modern treatment of the old inquiry "What is real?" It is my experience that busyness is all too often counterfeit success. This is especially true of *chronic busyness.* Busyness can start out okay, but if it is unchecked, we can get too busy to see what is really happening. With chronic busyness, we end up too busy for everything that is important. Our friendships are conducted only on Facebook. Dating is practical only if it is speed dating. Our partner keeps busy because we are so busy. Our children compete with our BlackBerry for our attention.

Chronic busyness keeps you estranged from the real you. Your success might look like success, but it doesn't feel like success. That's because it's not real success. A mantra I often share in my seminars on Success Intelligence is "If your definition of success has little or no measure of love in it, get another definition."[9] If you examine your true personal values, you will find traces of love in them all. Love is your real mind. "Let yourself be silently drawn by the stronger pull of what you really love,"[10] said Rumi. Love is creative. Steve Jobs, co-founder of Apple, was a modern mystic. He said, "The only way to do great work is to love what you do."[11]

Love is not just an enabler for success; love *is* success. The real work of your life is to know how to love and be loved. There is no greater work than this. Challenge this if you want. What is a higher expression of humanity than love? What is more inspiring than love? Politics is great, but only when leaders such as Nelson Mandela or Mahatma Gandhi infuse their politics with love. The same is true for leaders in science, economics, religion, business, and art.

> *"My favorite occupation is loving."*
>
> **Marcel Proust**

Love is the heart of success. And the real work of your life is to express your love. In my book *Authentic Success* (formerly titled *Success Intelligence*), I tell the story of the time a journalist asked me to sum up the heart of success in 100 words or less. I wrote something called the Love Dedication. I think it is fitting to include here:

Before you dedicate your life
to a person, a marriage, a family;
to a corporation, a political party,
a peace campaign;
to a religion, a revolution, a
spiritual path;
make one other dedication first.
First dedicate yourself to LOVE.
Decide to let Love be your
intention, your purpose, and
your point.
And then let Love inspire you,
support you, and guide you
in every other dedication
you make thereafter.[12]

All That You Want

Raymond Carver was one of America's best-loved poets and short-story writers of the 20th century. He died of lung cancer at the age of 50. Shortly before his death, he wrote "Late Fragment," which is inscribed on his tombstone at Ocean View Cemetery in Port Angeles. It reads:

And did you get what
you wanted from this life, even so?
I did.
And what did you want?
To call myself beloved, to feel myself
beloved on the earth.[13]

Our busy lives are full of desire. It looks like we want different things. "To each their own," the saying goes. It's not like that really, though. In truth, we want the same thing. What's different is that we each have separate strategies and plans for getting what we want. These strategies and plans can keep us busy as the years go on. By the middle of our lives we have probably forgotten what they were for. This forgetfulness causes us to feel tired and empty. We experience the pains of sleep. We only wake up when we remember that what we really wanted was to love and be loved.

The basic fear "I am not loveable" induces all sorts of cravings. It starts with looking for love, and when that doesn't work, we take whatever we can get. All the major life goals are really plays for love. We don't often admit this to each other or to ourselves. Basically, we are so terrified of not experiencing love that we make it look like we don't need it. So convincing are we that most of the major psychology studies on motivation theory and life goals have no entry for love in their indexes. We busy ourselves instead with pursuing happiness, chasing success, making money, being beautiful, winning respect, making our power plays, and getting the applause. And why do we do it? We do it to feel good. We do it for love.

We all need to feel loveable. It is our entry ticket into life. We can't show up properly without it. Feeling loveable helps you to be the real you, not an imitation. Feeling loveable connects you to the wisdom of your heart. This love brings out the best in you. But most of all, and this really is the key, feeling loveable is what enables you to love and be loved. That's why Raymond Carver

> *"Love Itself is all that you want."*
> **Ramana Maharshi**

didn't just want to feel "beloved" in some faraway heaven; he wanted to experience that eternal loveliness here. And he did. For ten years he experienced "Gravy," which was his word (and title of his poem) for the joy of loving and being loved.

The only thing of any real value in any situation is love. When you know this is true, all other cravings cease. Now you can stand firm in your true power. Dramas don't knock you off-center like before. You are not so easily distracted. You know what is real and what isn't. What matters most is being a more loving person. As you dedicate yourself to love, you are naturally happier, success comes more easily, and you attract great things, including love. When all you really want is love, you experience more of what you really want.

"When you want only love you will see nothing else."

A Course in Miracles[14]

♥ Chapter 17 ♥

A Call for Love

In the Loveability program I teach a module called "A Call for Love." This is the module that explores the relationship between love and forgiveness. To introduce this module, I share a passage from one of my favorite lessons in *A Course in Miracles*. The lesson is entitled "Forgiveness offers everything I want." It begins:

> What could you want forgiveness cannot give? Do you want peace? Forgiveness offers it. Do you want happiness, a quiet mind, a certainty of purpose, and a sense of worth and beauty that transcends the world? Do you want care and safety, and the warmth of sure protection always? Do you want a quietness that cannot be disturbed, a gentleness that never can be hurt, a deep, abiding comfort, and a rest so perfect it can never be upset?
>
> All this forgiveness offers you, and more. It sparkles on your eyes as you awake, and gives you joy with which to meet the day. It soothes your forehead while you sleep, and rests upon your eyelids so you see no dreams of fear and evil, malice and attack. And when you wake again, it offers you another day of happiness and peace. All this forgiveness offers you, and more.[1]

The Call for Love module happens at the midpoint of the Loveability program. I believe it's the most important module I teach. It is the heart of Loveability. The conversations and practices we do in this module have inspired some of the most beautiful healings and breakthroughs for my students. I remain in awe at what the miracle of forgiveness can do for us.

In the world we have made, it seems that there is too much hate and conflict for love to be real or to make any real difference. Growing up in this world, we encounter separation and fear so early on that our memory of love fades quickly. Searching the world for love, we meet so much pain and projection in our relationships that love feels like an impossible dream. All our efforts to love and be loved appear to be in vain, and this would be the story of this world if it weren't for one thing. Forgiveness is the difference between illusions and truth. Forgiveness undoes the blocks to love. Forgiveness restores the memory of love. Forgiveness is our salvation.

Healing the Basic Fear

When I first thought about forgiveness, I focused mostly on my relationships with others. I had resorted to forgiveness in the hopes that, by some miracle, it would take away the pain and injustice I felt at being treated unfairly. I wasn't sure exactly how forgiveness was going to do this, but it was worth a try. My early efforts at forgiveness didn't work very well. I could forgive, but I couldn't forget. Deep down I knew that forgiveness must be better than that. Over time, I changed my mind about forgiveness. Instead of focusing on others, I focused on me. Eventually I came to realize that *forgiveness is a decision you make to have a loving relationship with yourself.*

Self-forgiveness is about healing the basic fear "I am not loveable." This basic fear, as we have seen, is the primary cause of all the pain you experience in your relationships with parents, friends, lovers, and children. If you could forgive this basic fear, you wouldn't be hurt by anyone ever again, *nor would you cause any pain to others.* The first time you say, "I forgive myself for believing I am unloveable," it feels like nothing real has happened. The truth is, however, you have taken the first step to freeing yourself from a mind-set of fear and guilt that blocks your best efforts to love and be loved.

Guilt is a block to loving yourself and others. It also denies your right to any forgiveness. Essentially, there are two types of guilt. One is the "conscience guilt" you feel when you are unloving, unkind, or hurtful to someone. Your guilty conscience tells you that you have done something wrong. Your unloving actions cause you to feel unloveable. The other type of guilt is "identity guilt," which is what you feel when you believe the fear "I am unloveable." This identity guilt robs you of the memory of who you are and what love is.

When *guilt* and *fear* team up with *judgment,* you are at the mercy of an unholy trinity that causes you to believe "There is something wrong with me." When you identify with this guilty belief, you create an ego self-image that doesn't feel worthy of true love. Your ego encourages you to search for love, but it also tells you to hide from it when it approaches. With identity guilt, you are

> *"Love and guilt cannot coexist."*
>
> A Course in Miracles

afraid that if love finds you, it will see something unloveable. In this insane nightmare, the roles are reversed; love is the judge, and fear and guilt are your protectors. Even your ego can see that its best thinking can't help you now. Forgiveness is an angel you pray to when you need a miracle to save you.

Forgiveness invites you to change your mind about yourself. It encourages you to accept that although the ego feels guilty as hell, there is nothing wrong with the essence of who you are. Yes, you may have made mistakes in the past, but you are not your mistakes. Yes, you may be suffering from psychology, but you are not your thoughts. Yes, your personality may be neurotic and auditioning for a part in *High Anxiety,* but you are not your personality. Yes, your mother was a martyr and your father failed his emotional intelligence exam (and the re-test too), but that has nothing to do with who you really are.

Forgiveness reminds you that *nothing in the universe thinks there is anything wrong with you.* God is unconditional love, and so there is no karma between you and God. Heaven knows who you are, and the angels have not once fallen for your dreams of sin and guilt. The sun and the moon pour their light on you without any hesitation. Mother Earth and all her plants and trees give life to you without a trace of judgment. The birds and squirrels in the trees have never said a bad word about you. The dolphins and whales sing their songs of love to you and condemn you not. Guilt is an invention of egos and of human psychology. It exists nowhere else in the universe. Forgiveness reminds you of this, and also of your loving nature.

Each time you affirm "I forgive myself for believing I am unloveable," you are undoing the guilty self-image you made. This is a good thing for everyone. When you believe "I am unloveable," you project this judgment onto others, you attract relationships that play out guilt, and you end up accusing others of making you feel unloveable. In this "unforgiveable situation" you both try to establish your innocence by proving how wrong the other one is. This is the ego's attempt at justice. The winner wears the face of innocence but does not feel innocent inside. Guilt cannot establish innocence. Only forgiveness can do that, because forgiveness is a return to love.

I know there is a theory that humans need guilt, but this theory does not pass the test of truth or common sense. People who hold to this theory say that guilt is our conscience and that humans need a conscience. I agree that we need a conscience, but I believe we already had a conscience before guilt existed. *Guilt is not your real conscience; love is your real conscience.* When you pass your decisions and actions through the *conscience of love,* you realize that love is wise. It knows that what you do to others, you do to yourself. Love is ethical. It knows the difference between right and wrong. Love knows that, as you forgive, you are freed again to be a truly loving person in this world.

Seeing Things Differently

I have enjoyed a dialogue on forgiveness with my friend and mentor Tom Carpenter for more than 15 years now[2] and he has taught me so much about forgiveness. In the beginning, I repeatedly asked Tom, "What is forgiveness?" Thanks to Tom's patient tutelage, I came to see that forgiveness, like love, is not just a word, an idea, or even an occasional remedy. More than this, forgiveness is an attitude you approach each moment with. Forgiveness is a training in vision that helps you to see everything as it really is.

Forgiveness recognizes that everything you experience in this world is either *an expression of love or a call for love*. At the most basic level, your Unconditioned Self is an expression of love. Love is your spiritual DNA. Love is the consciousness of your soul. When you align your awareness with the basic truth "I am loveable," all your thoughts and actions are an expression of love. You experience a natural self-confidence. You are naturally kind and compassionate. You are a friend to everyone you meet. You know how to love and be loved. There is no big effort in any of this. You are the presence of love.

Forgiveness sees your ego as a call for love. Remember, the ego is not your Unconditioned Self; it is the self-image you make up in childhood and in later years. The basic fear of every ego is "I am not loveable." When you feel unloveable, you attack yourself with judgments like "I'm not good enough," you feel insecure, and you are vulnerable to feelings of unworthiness and insignificance. The psychology of your ego is a sign that you are *out of your mind* and you need help—in other words, a call for love. By affirming "I forgive myself for believing I

> *"Love always answers, being unable to deny a call for help."*
>
> A Course in Miracles

am unloveable," you call upon love to restore your sight and bring you back to your true self.

Throughout your day, you experience either expressions of love or calls for love. For instance, when you are chronically busy and have no time for yourself, this is a call for love; when the pace of your life is so hectic that it leaves you breathless, this is a call for love; or when you feel lonely and afraid that you won't find love, this is a call for love. Similarly, when you feel stuck and inspiration appears to have deserted you, this is a call for love; when you are tired and have nothing left to give, this is a call for love; or when you get sick, this too is a call for love. By contrast, an expression of love might be to stop and recognize how you could be more authentic, kind, and loving to yourself.

Forgiveness sees all communication as either an expression of love or a call for love. When you are aligned with your Unconditioned Self, you relate naturally and easily with others. People feel your love. They enjoy your company. You are a safe haven. Conversely, when you show up as an ego, the calls for love start to appear. For example, you put on a happy face (which everyone sees through), you toughen up (which fools nobody), you try to please people (which annoys everyone), you go into sacrifice (which scares everyone), you feel misunderstood (which no one acknowledges), you need your space (which is fine by everyone), and you wonder what's wrong with everyone today. These calls for love are a sign that it's time to reset yourself and to choose love again.

Every conflict is a call for love, according to forgiveness. At the highest level, the call for love is to remember what is true. Forgiveness recognizes that when two egos are in a fight, nothing real is threatened. The love that you are, and that joins you as one, is not diminished or lost; it is only forgotten temporarily. Forgiveness encourages you to hold your relationship in love so that you remember what your real goal is. For example, do you want fear or love, peace or conflict, happiness or pain? Forgiveness asks you to drop the attack so that you can see what the real need is. Thus, forgiveness helps you to remember who you are and to trust that love is always stronger than fear.

Letting Go of Grievances

Forgiveness can feel difficult to do. One reason for this is that we only give forgiveness serious consideration after something "unforgiveable" has happened to us. Typically, our practice of forgiveness does not start with minor grievances. Another reason is that we carry many misconceptions about what forgiveness is. We confuse forgiveness with sacrifice, for example. We believe forgiveness asks us to be charitable while we suffer in silence. We think forgiveness asks us to turn a blind eye and to refrain from trying to right a wrong. We fear that forgiveness asks too much of us. And so we cannot see that forgiveness offers us everything we want.

Anyone who has a past knows what a grievance is. I haven't met a man or woman who hasn't had to reconcile grievances from the past. What is a grievance? The *Oxford English Dictionary* describes a grievance as "a real or imaginary wrong causing resentment and regarded as grounds for complaint." We can all relate to the pain of being wronged. We've all experienced what we judge to be an injustice or wrongdoing. We have also acted grievously to others in the past. Our own wrongdoing is part of our wounding. Our history is full of grievances, then, but it is also, thank God, full of the healing of grievances.

Forgiveness is the process by which you let love replace all grievances. The first step in forgiving a grievance is to let yourself grieve. If someone you love has betrayed you, for example, you will understandably feel sad and angry. When a friend attacks you, or when you attack a friend, you will feel pain and hurt. When a relationship ends, for whatever reason, your disappointment is natural. Even when both people want to divorce, for example, there is still mourning for the passing of the old form of the relationship. When someone you love dies, it is essential to mourn well so that you can honor the past and commit to the future.

According to forgiveness, grief is a call for love. Forgiveness encourages you to respond lovingly to your grief. Forgiveness asks you to love yourself at this time. It wants you to give yourself permission to grieve and to be confident that your grieving will help you to heal. When you stop judging grief, you see that grief is not bad, wrong, or negative; it is simply part of the process of letting love heal. Forgiveness also asks you to let yourself be loved through this grieving process. This is a time to let your friends love you. This is a time for prayer. It is a time to be with God. It is a time to pray with Jesus, to meditate with Buddha, and to allow for all manner of grace and spiritual inspiration.

Forgiveness recognizes that if you don't let yourself grieve properly, there is no end to the grieving. However, when you grieve properly, it brings you to a moment—a holy moment—when you can now let the grieving go. I call this a holy moment because it is a time of transition in the forgiveness process. In this transition you experience an *inner shift* in which you start to see yourself differently, others differently, and also your past differently. In your mind you walk across a bridge that takes you from the past into the present. As you keep walking across this bridge, you let go of everything about you that is not love. Eventually, as you step off this bridge, you are born into a full awareness of what love is.

As you get ready to let go of your grievances, you will experience one last temptation. Can you guess what this final temptation is? It is to hold on to the grievances for a little longer. This temptation arises because you still cling to an old belief that grievances offer something valuable to you. Even though the burden of carrying these grievances has brought you to your knees countless times, you still hope they might right a wrong. These grievances have promised you a victory, but the pain of this victory is too much to bear. Now is the moment to call on love's awareness to help you see through this miserable righteousness.

This final temptation falls away when you let yourself see the folly of carrying grievances. Here are five principles I teach my students in the Loveability program.

1. Love holds no grievances: "You who were created by love like itself can hold no grievances and know your Self. To hold a grievance is to forget who you are," says *A Course in Miracles*.[3] You cannot hold on to a grievance and feel the love that is your true nature. So, instead of being the presence of love, you play a parody of your true Self. You act like a victim. You are quick to point out the errors of others but not your own. The real error is that you have forgotten who you are. Grievances are a sign of a mistaken identity. With forgiveness, your victim identity dissolves and eventually there is nothing left of you except love.

2. Grievances are made of fear: When you hold on to grievances, your thinking is dominated by fear. You hesitate to let your grievances go, because you're afraid this will make you even unhappier than you already are. You mistakenly believe that carrying grievances soothes your pain and that letting them go would hurt you. The truth is that when you carry a grievance, *you are hurting yourself in an effort to gain revenge or justice.* Grievances hurt the one who is aggrieved, just as forgiveness heals the one who forgives. All that you do to others, you do also to yourself. Forgiveness heals fear.

3. Grievances are not a solution: "You can be as mad as a mad dog at the way things went. You could swear, curse the Fates, but when it comes to the end, you have to let go," says Benjamin Button in the film *The Curious Case of Benjamin Button*. It's hard not to have wishes and hopes for how things should work out and not to feel aggrieved when things don't go according to our plans. However, after you have grieved, you have to let go, otherwise you are arguing with reality. No amount of anger changes the past. Being guilty forever won't heal anything or anyone. Trying to make others feel guilty won't give you peace.

4. Grievances hold you back: What you do not heal in your past will show up in your present relationships and in the life you live now. It doesn't matter how often you change your cast or your location; the story will be the same until you forgive. Without forgiveness, the past can turn up at any moment, and you will repeat your history. However, forgiveness can change your past and the present by helping you give it a different purpose. *The purpose of your life is not to carry a grievance.* With forgiveness, you can grieve and then ask love to help you use the past to create a future that moves in the direction of love.

5. Grievances don't make you happy: Sometimes we hold on to grievances because we are afraid that our past was our best chance for happiness. However, you can't continue to carry a grievance and hope to be happy. To be truly happy, you have to be willing to make love more important than your grievances, your ego, and your past. There comes a time, then, when you have to accept that every grievance has an expiration date. By being willing to forgive, you come to see that there is life after a grievance.

The Buddha asked us to offer loving kindness to the whole world, including our enemies. Jesus asked us to love our enemies.[4] He asked us to forgive the world. Why love this much? Why forgive anything? The way I see it, we don't forgive in order to be nice, to do what we should, to be good Christians, or even to be spiritual. We forgive so as to set ourselves free. Forgiveness helps us to see beyond our masks to who we truly are. It shows us that who we really are has nothing to do with what happened to us in the past. "No one has ever been angry at another human being— we're only angry at our story of them," writes Byron Katie, author of *Loving What Is.*[5] When you love your enemies, you have no enemies. When you love your sins, your sins are washed away. Forgiveness helps us to feel like our true selves again. Forgiveness helps us to love and be loved once more.

Dear God, I declare a day of amnesty
in which I gratefully volunteer to hand in all
my resentments and grievances to You.
Please help me to handle well all the
peace, love, happiness, and success
that must inevitably follow.
Amen.

♥ **Chapter 18** ♥

The Presence
of Love

I packed a suitcase full of books for my retreat on Mount Athos. My friend Andy had told me not to bother bringing a computer or anything that needed a plug. "Only the top monks have Internet access," he said. Apparently, I'd also need to brush up on my ancient Greek and Latin if I wanted to read the books in the monastery library. After I'd found my big, soft rock on that first morning on Mount Athos, I was so absorbed in my meditations and in writing in my journal that I completely forgot about the books I came with. There was something in the air on the Holy Mountain that made me want just to sit, be still, and listen.

On my third day on Mount Athos, just before sunset, I was in my dormitory searching in my suitcase for another journal—I'd already filled up two—when I noticed a book lying under my bed. I bent down and picked it up and saw that it was one I had brought with me. It must have fallen out of my suitcase. The book was *The Art of Loving* by Erich Fromm.[1] *The Art of Loving* was a book I'd been meaning to read for ages. My mum had given it to me as a birthday present. She knew how much I'd enjoyed reading *The Art of Being* and *The Art of Listening,* also by Erich Fromm. I had planned to read it as soon as I was given it, but the time had never been right. Not until that moment.

When I read a book, I like to underline the good bits. With *The Art of Loving,* I pretty much underlined everything. *The Art of Loving* is a short book, only 129 pages long. It's not a quick read, though. Fromm starts with two questions. He writes, "Is love an art? Then it requires knowledge and effort. Or is love a pleasant sensation, which to experience is a matter of chance, something one 'falls into' if one is lucky?"[2] He answers his own questions by saying that love is an art that requires character, courage, discipline, and patience. He describes love as the "ultimate and real need in every human being."[3] Moreover, he sees love as "the answer to the problem of human existence."[4] In conclusion, he tells us:

> If it is true, as I have tried to show, that love is *the only sane and satisfactory answer to the problem of human existence,* then any society which excludes, relatively, the development of love, must in the long run perish of its own contradiction with the basic necessities of human nature.[5]

The Art of Loving had an enormous impact on me. Many times previously, I had read philosophers and poets, saints and mystics, who attested that love is our salvation and enlightenment. However, this was the first time I had read this idea expressed by a Western psychologist and political activist, a man judged to be one of the most important intellectuals of the 20th century. "Without love, humanity could not exist for a day," said Fromm.[6] He also asserted that, without love, we cannot be free, that society cannot function in a sane way, and that humanity will attack and destroy itself.

> *"The salvation of man is through love and in love."*
>
> **Viktor Frankl**

As I sat on my big, soft rock for the last time on my retreat on Mount Athos, I reflected on Erich Fromm's assertion that love is "the answer to the problem of human existence." The angle of the afternoon sun and the light breeze in the air had turned the Aegean Sea into an ocean of diamonds.

Can love save the world? I wondered.

As I mulled the question over, I could feel a pull toward both "Yes" and "No." As I thought about it more, I realized that it's too soon to say that love can't save the world, because we haven't tried it yet. Also, given the state of the world today, it's already too late just to think about such things. Therefore, a better question to ask is "How can love save the world?" And better still, "How can my love help to save the world?"

A Problem Solved

Erich Fromm said that love is the answer to "the problem" of human existence. Notably, he didn't say "the problems" of human existence. His lifetime study of the human psyche and its pathology revealed to him that all our problems are caused by one basic problem. The basic problem is separateness. "Man—of all ages and cultures—is confronted with the solution of one and the same question: the question of how to overcome separateness, how to achieve union, how to transcend one's own individual life and find atonement," wrote Fromm in *The Art of Loving.*[7]

The basic problem of separation begins in the *first degree* with a feeling of separation from our Unconditioned Self and from the basic truth "I am loveable." This feeling of separateness is our fall from grace. It gives rise to the basic fear "I am not loveable." When we identify with this fear, we experience a mindset that Fromm describes as "a prison of aloneness" and "the source of all anxiety," which "arouses shame and feelings of guilt." We experience a loss of harmony within. We are not comfortable in our own skin. We cannot feel our own heart. We experience what Meister Eckhart called "a storm of inward thought."[8]

> *"The deepest need of man, then, is the need to overcome his separateness, to leave the prison of his aloneness. The absolute failure to achieve this aim means insanity . . ."*

> **Erich Fromm,** *The Art of Loving*[9]

The basic problem of separation in the *second degree* is experienced as a loss of harmony and connection with others. The basic fear "I am not loveable" gives rise to judgment and unworthiness, which you try to contain inside yourself, but which is always projected outward onto others. You don't mean for this to happen, but it does. Your loved ones feel it when you are estranged from your *eternal loveliness.* You make it difficult to be loved when you negate yourself. Your efforts to love others unconditionally are defeated by your lack of self-acceptance. Hence, the basic fear "I am not loveable," as felt in the *first degree* of separation, is now experienced in the *second degree* as "You don't love me" and "We can't love each other."

The basic problem of separation in the *third degree* is mirrored in our relationship with the world. In other words, all our so-called worldly problems are just symptoms of the one basic problem. Can you see the link? The fall from grace from your Unconditioned Self causes you to feel out of place in the world. The basic fear "I am not loveable" then gives rise to paranoid thoughts that "the world does not love me" and "the world is not a loving place." The alienation from your loving nature gives rise to a *human destructiveness,* a term coined by Fromm that causes competition, greed, poverty, famine, racism, violence, and war. Hence separation as experienced in the first, second, and third degree causes a world full of problems.

> *"The love in one of us is the love in all of us."*
>
> **Marianne Williamson**

And now for some good news! *The basic problem of human existence is not real.* Separateness is a trick of perception that mystics have seen through since the beginning of time. "In the Yoga of Love we see that matter and spirit are one. It's only the ego that separates," said Ramana Maharshi.[10] Separateness is an optical delusion that modern physicists have now proven to be unreal. "Quantum physics thus reveals a basic oneness of the universe," declared Erwin Schrödinger.[11] What is the conclusion to all of this? It's that the problem of separation has already been solved. The separation from our Unconditioned Self never happened. The separateness we experience between each other is a mistake. What blocks our efforts to love and be loved is not real.

On Love's Path

During my retreat at the monastery on Mount Athos, I met a monk named Alexis, whose job it is to coordinate world prayers. Alexis keeps a roster that ensures there is always at least one monk in the chapel praying prayers for the whole world. This roster operates both day and night. Alexis describes his job as "a service of love." He told me that the same thing happens in each of the 20 monasteries on Mount Athos. I have witnessed similar prayer vigils in temples, churches, ashrams, mosques, and synagogues on my travels. All over the world, right at this moment, there are Buddhists, Christians, Hindus, Muslims, Jews, and people of no religion praying for the world and praying for you.

When I was a young child, I prayed for the world every night. I had forgotten about this until recently, when my mother reminded me of it. She remembers it like yesterday. As she began to describe my bedtime ritual, the memories came flooding back to me. She told me how I made her and Dad promise solemnly to make sure I never skipped my prayers. They were also under orders to wake me up if I ever fell asleep before saying my prayers. Sometimes I would make Mum and Dad say the prayers with me. Mum and Dad were not religious. We didn't go to church. This wasn't something I learned to do. I just did it. Mum even remembers the prayer I said. It goes:

God bless all the mummies and daddies.
God bless all the children and animals.
God bless all the trees and flowers.
God bless everyone and everything.
Thank you, God, for your blessings.
Amen.

What is it that moves a child to pray for the world? What is it that makes us want to pray for people we have not met and are never likely to? I believe it's because we know, in our hearts, that we are all on a path of love. We know that, although our lives appear to take us in different directions, we are on the same journey. We also know that the shared purpose of our lives is to love and be loved. We know that everything we experience here is a lesson in love. We know that love is the creative principle that helps us to grow and evolve. We know that we are all here to help move the world in the direction of love.

We pray for each other, and extend love to each other, because it is natural to do so. Love is our true nature. It is the will of Creation. It is the shared will of God and our Unconditioned Self. To love is to be who we are. It is our natural expression, our basic instinct. We love without thinking about it. We love because our hearts want to. There is no force in any of this. There is no sacrifice either. There are many reasons to love, but mostly we love because it is our joy to do so. Birds sing, dolphins leap, dogs chase their tails, flowers bloom, trees offer their fruit, and we love each other because we like to.

> *"Love is the natural human inclination."*
>
> **Ram Dass**

Love is an attitude of oneness. Love reminds us that we all exist in the same neighborhood. We are made of the same love. Men and women are made of the same love. Muslims and Christians are made of the same love. Democrats and Republicans are made of the same love. In the detour into fear, we tried to make love special and to withhold love from people who appear different to us—from another religion, another race, another caste, and another class. The more we tried to love just a *few chosen people,* though, the more impossible it got. We couldn't love our loved ones. We couldn't even love ourselves. The message of love is that *you can't love someone if you are not willing to love everyone.*

"Love is not primarily a relationship to a specific person," writes Fromm in *The Art of Loving;* "it is an *attitude,* an *orientation of character* which determines the relatedness of a person to the world as a whole, not toward one 'object' of love. If a person loves only one other person and is indifferent to the rest of his fellow men, his love is not love but a symbiotic attachment, or an enlarged egotism."[12] Later on in the same paragraph, he writes, "If I truly love one person I love all persons, I love the world, I love life. If I can say to somebody else, 'I love you,' I must be able to say, 'I love in you everybody, I love through you the world, I love in you also myself.'"[13]

A Daily Practice

> **I know the way you can get**
> **When you have not had a drink of Love:**
>
> **Your face hardens,**
> **Your sweet muscles cramp.**
> **Children become concerned**
> **About a strange look that appears in your eyes**
> **Which even begins to worry your own mirror**
> **And nose.**
>
> **Squirrels and birds sense your sadness**
> **And call an important conference in a tall tree.**
> **They decide which secret code to chant**
> **To help your mind and soul.**[14]

In these opening verses of Hafiz's poem "I Know the Way You Can Get," he warns us that we must make love a daily practice, and not just an occasional thing, if we are to deny the illusion of separation and fear. In the Loveability program I encourage my students to commit to love as a daily practice. We support each other in recognizing what helps us to tune in to the presence of love and to be a loving presence in the world. To this end, I share from my holy bag a wonderful mix of attunements, meditations, inquiries, and activities that help me in my daily practice on love's path. Here are a few examples:

Attunement: "100 Breaths" is an attunement practice I do every day, and it's usually the first exercise I share in the Loveability program. The idea is to dedicate 100 breaths to love. With each breath, you let yourself open up to the presence of love and you let love reveal itself to you. You tune in to a love that is already here, that is infinite, that is all-inclusive, that is constant, and that is everywhere. You did not make this love. It made you. This love is here for you and it will bless you, guide you, and inspire you if you let it.

Dedication: The practice of dedicating your day to love is a surrender to love. By affirming "I dedicate today to love," you invite love to be in charge of your relationships, your work, your plans, and everything about your day. There are many wonderful practices for consecrating your day. The Prayer of St. Francis is a personal favorite. James Twyman and Sarah McLachlan have both set this prayer to music. In *A Course in Miracles,* one of the lessons is: "Today belongs to love. Let me not fear." In my yoga practice, I regularly do the Heart Salutation (Hridaya Namaskar) taught to me by Shiva Rea. I often listen to the Heart Sutra Mantra sung by Krishna Das and by Deva Premal. Most days, I visit the Facebook page for The Forgiveness Network, and I also read Mastin Kipp's blog *The Daily Love.*

Inquiry: One way to practice inquiry is to choose a question as a focus for your day. You can start the day in meditation with a question. You can take this question with you as you go through your day. And then you can reflect on your question at the end of the day. Here are some examples of inquiries on love:

"How can I be a more loving person?"
"How can I be warmer?"
"How can I be more considerate?"
"How can I be more compassionate?"

"How can I be more romantic?"
"How can I be kinder?"

Meditations: The Tibetan Buddhist practice of Metta Bhavana, or Loving Kindness, is a meditation I do daily.[15] There are five parts to the Loving Kindness practice. In part one, you offer unconditional love to yourself. This helps you to cultivate compassion for yourself and also to extend unconditional love to others. In part two, you extend unconditional love to a loved one. This helps to cultivate appreciation. In part three, you extend unconditional love to a stranger. This helps to cultivate generosity. In part four, you extend love to someone you are having difficulty with. This helps to cultivate forgiveness. In part five, you extend love to the whole world. This helps to cultivate a feeling of oneness.

Creativity: While writing this book, I did an art project in which I created 50 oil paintings. Each painting was of a heart and of a particular quality of the heart, like gratitude, kindness, compassion, forgiveness, and oneness. These paintings were part of my daily attunement to love, and they helped me to write this book. There is a beautiful reciprocity between creativity and love. Love is creative, and creativity helps us to express our love. It is said that love can make an artist out of anyone. Find your artistry. If you love to cook, cook with love. If you love to garden, give your green fingers some exercise. If you love to sing, sing with love. Do what you love to do, and do it with love.

Actions: To make love a daily practice, do something every day that helps you to remember that love is your true nature. Meditate. Pray. Dance. Volunteer. Donate. Serve. Speak up. Listen to the Voice of Love and know that it is God's voice. Trust the Voice of Love and know that it is your voice. Act in love, and in the ways of love. The poet William Martin says, "Make it your daily discipline to lay aside one little thing; a tiny fear, a simple preoccupation, a useless book, a piece of household clutter, a habit of avoidance, a bit of shame and guilt, a desire that distracts, and what will be left is Love Itself."[16]

A Time for Love

We have a basic choice to make. This basic choice influences every other choice we make. The basic choice is love.

To choose love is not a small thing. It is to accept that love is your true nature. It is to surrender to your highest calling. To choose love is to admit that love is what you really want. It meansthat that you are willing to make love a priority in your life. It means you are ready to be open to love, to trust in love, and to make way for love.

The choice for love presents itself to you every day. It is the basic spiritual practice of your life. To choose love is to recognize that life is all about love and that even when it isn't, it still is, really. Love is always relevant and there is not a moment in your day that is not about love. To choose love is to be receptive to love in every situation. It is to see that love is the highest purpose of every relationship. It is to let your work be an expression of love, and your play and recreation, too.

> *"The aim of all spiritual practice is love."*
>
> **Sai Baba**

To choose love is to bring more love into your conversations, especially the difficult ones. Love is the courage to talk about what matters most. Trust in love and know that love can handle a difficult conversation. There is a place for love always, and love can make a difference. Let love guide you. Know that love is listening. Know that love will tell you when to speak and what to say. To choose love is the smart thing to do. Love is not passive. Love will use you, if you are willing. To choose love is to say, "I am willing to be a loving presence here." To be a loving presence is the greatest and most helpful contribution you can make to any situation.

Is love really enough? The answer is "No" if you still want to believe that love is outside of you and that you and the world are two separate things. Love is not enough if love is just a nice idea or a positive mental attitude. Love cannot help you, and it cannot save the world, if you won't accept that love is your essence. The answer is "Yes," however, if you accept that you are one with love and one with the world. Now you can call on something bigger than your ego's best efforts. Now you have access to your true power, which is our shared power, and also the power of God. To choose love is to bring the intelligence of the universe into play.

You cannot know the power of love until you choose love. So, choose love, and notice what happens. First, notice what happens to you. Notice how your body is free of fear, your heart is free of guilt, and your mind is free of judgment. Next, notice what happens around you. Notice how your love touches others. Scientists are now able to measure how the activity of your heart resonates with the world.[17] They have measured how your loving actions have an influence of at least three degrees of separation,[18] which basically means that the effects of love travel farther than your eye can see. We live in a social network. We share the same sacred circuitry. That is why love is so powerful.

When you choose love, the world pays attention. For example, have you heard the story of Ronny? Ronny is 41 years old. He is a citizen of Israel. He is a father. He is a graphic designer. He is a teacher. Ronny grew concerned at the increasing threat of war between Israel and Iran. He felt in his heart that a war made no sense. But what could Ronny, a graphic designer, do about that? Ronny created a poster. It has a simple design, and it reads: "Iranians. We will never bomb your country. We love you." Ronny posted his poster on Facebook. He followed it up with a short video message to the people of Iran. This is what he said:

> To the Iranian people. To all the fathers, mothers, children, brothers, and sisters. For there to be a war between

us, first we must be afraid of each other. We must hate. I'm not afraid of you. I don't hate you. I don't even know you. No Iranian ever did me no harm. I never even met an Iranian. Just one in Paris in a museum. Nice dude . . . I see sometime here, on the TV, an Iranian. He is talking about war. I'm sure he does not represent all the people of Iran. If you see someone on your TV talking about bombing you, be sure he does not represent all of the people of Israel. To all those who feel the same, share this message and help it reach the Iranian people.[19]

Instantly, Ronny's poster was being shared on Facebook pages across the world. Inside 48 hours, Ronny had received posters created by Iranians that said, "We love you Israeli people. The people of Iran do not want any war with any country." Within a few weeks, over one million people had seen Ronny's message on YouTube. Over 100,000 people had "liked" his Facebook page. Ronny created a website (www.israelovesiran.com). The welcome message reads: "Creating a Bridge of Communication Between the People of the Middle East." There are links on the website to similar campaigns, such as "Iran loves Israel" and "America loves Iran and Israel" and "Germany loves Iran" and "Jews of World love Iran."

Can love stop a war? Can love end racial conflict? Can love end hunger and world poverty? Can love heal an ancient hatred? The answer to all these questions is "Yes." How does love do this? Love does this in exactly the same way that it helps you to stop attacking yourself, to let go of judgments, to heal guilt, and to practice forgiveness with your family and friends. First, love changes you. Love helps you to change your mind about yourself. It helps you to see yourself without fear, judgment, guilt, and lack. The basic fear "I am not loveable" disappears into love.

As you let love change you, the world changes, too. This must be so, because you and the world are connected. According to your ego and the illusion of separation, you play a small part in the world and only for a short time; but according to love and one-ness, the center of the world is everywhere and the world is in you, and so you will always have a big part to play. This shift in percep-tion is one of the effects of love. Love helps you to see that the world is an effect, not a cause. The world is the way it is because of who we have been pretending to be. As we remember who we re-ally are, the world is changed, and everything that is not love gradually disappears.

We can help each other to choose love. We do this by choos-ing to be a loving presence in each other's lives. We can also ask God to help us to choose love. We can ask love to help us too. Remember, *God* and *love* are the same experience dressed up in two different words (like with *you* and *I,* and *he* and *she,* and *us* and *them*). The interesting thing

> "In form you are the microcosm; in reality you are the macrocosm."
>
> **Rumi**

to note about the choice for love is that it's a choice your true self has made already. The essence of who you are has already chosen love. It is choosing love in every moment. And when you forget about love, it can help you to choose again.

The knowledge that your heart—and that everybody else's heart—has already made the choice for love is a big help in bring-ing the story of separation and fear to an end. Right now, we are here to love and be loved. This is what it means to be on love's path. This is what helps to move the world in the direction of love. This is how we find our way home.

To close, I leave you with a poem I wrote on the eve of my first Loveability program. It is called "Disappearing into Love."

**When they ask you what is your
religion, tell them that it is
love.**

And if they ask you what are your
politics, tell them that it is
also love.

If they ask you what that means,
you can tell them your
philosophy is love.

If they want to know anything
else about you, tell them your
favorite occupation is
loving.

And don't forget to tell them
that your nationality is
love.

And that even your blood
group is love.

Not everyone will stick around
to hear what you say next,
but fear not.

Family and friends may get busy
so as to pretend to forget what
you just said.

It'd drive them crazy now to know
that their blood group is also love,
that their nationality is love,
and that the real work of their
life is love.

One day they will give in, and then
their philosophy will be love,

their politics will be love,
and their religion will be love.

Love gets us all in the end.
We all of us disappear back into
love eventually.

♥ Loveability Library ♥

Here is a list of resources I recommend to students who attend my Loveability program.

Books

The Art of Extreme Self-Care, by Cheryl Richardson. Carlsbad, CA: Hay House, 2009.

The Art of Loving, by Erich Fromm. New York: HarperPerennial, 2000.

Be Love Now: The Path of the Heart, by Ram Dass. London: Rider, 2011.

Born for Love: Reflections on Loving, by Leo F. Buscaglia. New York: Fawcett, 1995.

A Course in Miracles, Combined Volume, Third Edition. Mill Valley, CA: Foundation for Inner Peace, 2007.

The Five Love Languages: The Secret to Love That Lasts, by Gary Chapman. Chicago: Moody Publishers, 2010.

If it Hurts, It Isn't Love, by Chuck Spezzano. New York: Marlowe & Co., 2000.

Love Always Answers, by Diane Berke. New York: Crossroad, 1994.

Love and Survival: The Scientific Basis for the Healing Power of Intimacy, by Dean Ornish. New York: HarperPerennial, 1999.

Love Is Letting Go of Fear, by Gerald G. Jampolsky, M.D. Berkeley, CA: Celestial Arts, 1982.

Love Is the Answer, by Gerald G. Jampolsky, M.D., and Diane V. Cirincione. New York: Bantam, 1991.

Lovingkindness: The Revolutionary Art of Happiness, by Sharon Salzberg. Boston: Shambhala, 2002.

Loving Relationships Treasury, by Sondra Ray. Berkeley, CA: Celestial Arts, 2006.

Loving What Is, by Byron Katie. London: Rider, 2002.

The Miracle of Real Forgiveness, by Tom Carpenter. Carpenter Press, 2010.

The Path to Love, by Deepak Chopra. New York: Three Rivers Press, 1997.

A Return to Love: Reflections on the Principles of "A Course in Miracles," by Marianne Williamson. New York: HarperCollins, 1992.

The Subject Tonight Is Love: 60 Wild and Sweet Poems of Hafiz, translated by Daniel Ladinsky. Pumpkin House Press, 1996.

True Love: A Practice for Awakening the Heart, by Thích Nhất Hạnh. Boston: Shambhala, 2006.

WE: Understanding the Psychology of Human Love, by Robert A. Johnson. San Francisco: HarperSanFrancisco, 1998.

Why Kindness Is Good for You, by David Hamilton. Carlsbad, CA: Hay House, 2010.

Audio

How to Love Yourself: Cherishing the Incredible Miracle That You Are (Audio CD), by Louise L. Hay. Carlsbad, CA: Hay House, 2006.

Lovingkindness Meditation (Audio CD), by Sharon Salzberg. Louisville, CO: Sounds True, 2005.

The Secret of Love: Meditations for Attracting and Being in Love (Audio CD), by Deepak Chopra. Monostereo, 2011.

DVD

Love & Emptiness (DVD), a talk by A. H. Almaas. Diamond Heart, 2004.

Blog & Facebook

The Daily Love, by Mastin Kipp, at www.thedailylove.com.

The Forgiveness Network, by Tom Carpenter, at www.facebook.com/theforgivenessnetwork.

❤ Acknowledgments ❤

Thank you, Hollie Holden, for your love and support. Our late-night conversations, after our babies had finally gone to sleep, breathed life into this book. Night after night, you sat at the kitchen table, baking fresh edits so I could write in the morning. It's been so much fun co-writing *Loveability* with you. Thank you to my daughter, Bo, for drawing the heart that appears on the cover of *Loveability,* and also for so many good stories to tell. And thank you to my son, Christopher, especially for all the times you say "I lubba daddy," "I lubba mummy," "I lubba Bo," and "I lubba ball."

Thank you to all my teachers. In particular, thank you, Tom and Linda Carpenter, Chuck and Lency Spezzano, and Don Riso and Russ Hudson. I have been inspired by many wonderful teachers, including Marianne Williamson, Louise Hay, Sondra Ray, Gerry Jampolsky, Byron Katie, Deepak Chopra, Erich Fromm, Ramana Maharshi, Rumi, and Hafiz (and Daniel Ladinsky).

Thank you to my family. Thank you to my father, Alex, and my mother, Sally, for loving me so beautifully. Thank you to my brother, David, for being a most wonderful brother. Thank you to Lizzie Prior, my sister-in-law, for a thousand creative contributions made to the Loveability program. Thank you to Miranda Macpherson for your love and inspiration. Thank you to Raina Nahar for being the "I AM LOVE" presence in our lives. Thank you to my Prior family for your love and support. Thank you to all my friends.

Thank you to everyone on the Loveability team. Thank you to Ian Lynch, Lizzie Prior (again), Avril Carson, Sue Boyd, Candy Constable, Helen Allen, Robert Norton, Ola Odumosu, Marianne Adjei, Saloni Singh, and Chris Morris. And thank you to all the students who have attended one of the Loveability public programs.

Thank you to Ben Renshaw for helping me to make the space to write this book. Thank you to Sabrina Jevtic for making sure the office ran smoothly while I was away. Thank you to Wendy Sears for your help with the research. Thank you to David Hamilton for your generous support with research on the science of love. Thank you also to Bruce Lipton for your help with the science of love. And thank you to Alla Svirinskaya for your support throughout the writing of *Loveability*.

Thank you to the Hay House team. Thank you to Louise Hay for being a loving presence in my life. Thank you to Reid Tracy for giving me such a rich canvas to paint on. Thank you to Patty Gift for being a wonderful friend and editor. Thank you also to Celia Fuller-Vels, Anne Barthel, Richelle Zizian, Laura Gray, Christy Salinas, Donna Abate, and Nancy Levin.

Thank you to the William Morris Agency, and especially to my agent, Jennifer Rudolph Walsh.

Amen.

❥ Endnotes ❥

PART I: LOVE IS YOUR DESTINY

1. "Search for Love," in *The Complete Poems of D. H. Lawrence* (Ware, Hertfordshire: Wordsworth Editions, 1994), p. 552.

2. *Doors of perception.* "If the doors of perception were cleansed every thing would appear to man as it is, infinite. For man has closed himself up, till he sees all things through narrow chinks of his cavern." William Blake, *The Marriage of Heaven and Hell* (Mineola, NY: Dover Publications, 1994), plate 14.

Chapter 1: Love Is Not a Word

1. *6,909 languages.* M. Paul Lewis, ed., *Ethnologue: Languages of the World,* 16th ed. (Dallas, TX: SIL International, 2009).

2. *Bo language.* Alastair Lawson, "Last speaker of ancient language of Bo dies in India," BBC News, February 4, 2010, http://news.bbc.co.uk/1/hi/world/south_asia/8498534.stm.

3. "The Good Root," in *The Rumi Collection,* ed. Kabir Helminski (Boston: Shambhala, 2000), p. 235.

4. "Only Love Can Explain Love," in *Teachings of Rumi,* by Andrew Harvey (Boston: Shambhala, 1999), p. 77.

5. Richard Feynman, *The Feynman Lectures on Physics,* rev. 50th anniversary ed., vol. 1 (New York: Basic Books, 2011), 4–1. Also see Richard Feynman in Wikiquote for a digest of inspiration.

6. "The Spring Also," in *The Soul of Rumi,* ed. Coleman Barks (San Francisco: HarperSanFrancisco, 2002), p. 225–226.

Chapter 2: Your Eternal Loveliness

1. *A lively flame.* My homage to the chapter "On the Wonderful Effect of Divine Love," in *The Imitation of Christ,* by Thomas Kempis (London: Penguin Classics, 2005). The description of love as a lively flame is also the inspiration for one of my favorite collections of love quotations: *A Lively Flame: Inspirations on Love and Relationships,* ed. Eileen Campbell (London: Thorsons, 1992).

2. *Original Face.* For further reading, visit http://en.wikipedia.org/wiki /Original_face.

3. *Original Blessing.* Read Matthew Fox, *Original Blessing: A Primer in Creation Spirituality,* 2nd rev. ed. (Rochester, VT: Bear & Company, 1996), and also Matthew Henry, ed., *Originally Blessed: The 25th Anniversary of Matthew Fox's "Original Blessing"* (Golden, CO: Creation Spirituality Communities, 2008).

4. Deepak Chopra, *The Path to Love* (New York: Three Rivers Press, 1997), p. 2.

5. Galway Kinnell, "Saint Francis and the Sow," in *Three Books* (New York: Houghton Mifflin, 2002).

6. "What Is the Body?" in *A Course in Miracles,* Workbook, Combined Volume, 3rd ed. (Mill Valley, CA: Foundation for Inner Peace, 2007), p. 425. *A Course in Miracles* combines perennial wisdom and spiritual psychology to teach you how to replace a mind-set of fear, judgment, and guilt with a mind-set of unconditional love.

Chapter 3: Our Shared Purpose

1. *Love and science.* Read Sue Gerhardt, *Why Love Matters: How Affection Shapes a Baby's Brain* (New York: Routledge, 2004); also David Hamilton, *Why Kindness Is Good for You* (Carlsbad, CA: Hay House, 2010); also Helen Fisher, *Why We Love: The Nature and Chemistry of Romantic Love* (New York: Henry Holt and Company, 2004).

2. *Love and animals.* American psychologist Harry Harlow is known for his research on rhesus monkeys. He famously said, "If monkeys have taught us anything it's that you've got to learn how to love before you learn how to live." In *This Week,* March 3, 1961. For more information, read Harry F. Harlow, "The Nature of Love," *American Psychologist* 13, no. 12 (December 1958), pp. 673–685.

Chapter 4: Ground of Love

1. Recommended reading: M. Scott Peck, "Love," chapter 2 in *The Road Less Travelled* (London: Rider Classics, 2008).

2. *Love and work*. Freud said, "The communal life of human beings had, therefore, a two-fold foundation: the compulsion to work, which was created by external necessity, and the power of love." Sigmund Freud, *Civilization and Its Discontents* (New York: Penguin Classics, 2004). Another version of this famous quote by Freud is "Love and work . . . work and love, that's all there is."

3. Sigmund Freud, *The Psychology of Love* (New York: Penguin Classics, 2006). Of love and madness, Plato said, "Love is a serious mental disease," and Nietzsche said, "There is always some madness in love."

4. Sigmund Freud, *On Narcissism: An Introduction* (New Haven, CT: Yale University Press, 1991).

5. Thierry Bokanowski and Sergio Lewkowicz, eds., *On Freud's "Splitting of the Ego in the Process of Defence"* (London: Karnac Books, 2009).

6. Stephen A. Mitchell and Jay R. Greenberg, *Object Relations in Psychoanalytic Theory* (Cambridge, MA: Harvard University Press, 1984).

7. *Hidden Ground of Love: The Letters of Thomas Merton on Religious Experience and Social Concerns*, ed. William H. Shannon (New York: Harcourt Brace Jovanovich, 1993).

8. "There is no love but God's," lesson 127 in *A Course in Miracles*, p. 230.

9. From a letter Einstein wrote in 1950, quoted in Walter Sullivan, "The Einstein Papers: A Man of Many Parts," *The New York Times*, March 29, 1972.

Chapter 5: Live Your Love

1. *Birmingham City University*. When I attended it was called Birmingham Polytechnic. In 1992 it changed its name to University of Central England in Birmingham. The name Birmingham City University was announced in 2007.

2. Juan Mascaró, trans., *The Bhagavad Gita* (London: Penguin, 2003).

3. Paramahansa Yogananda, *Autobiography of a Yogi* (Los Angeles: Self-Realization Fellowship, 2006).

4. Quoted in Sant Tukaram, *Love Is the Door, Chanting Is the Key: An Introduction to Kirtan & Bhakti Yoga Sadhana*, available for free download online at www .himalayanheritage.org/publications/loveisthedoor.

5. *Path with heart*. A reference to the dialogue in Carlos Castaneda, *The Teachings of Don Juan* (London: Arkana, 1990), in which Don Juan says, "Does this path have a heart? If it does, the path is good; if it doesn't it is of no use."

6. "The Function of Time," chapter 13, verse 4, in *A Course in Miracles*, p. 245.

7. "Atonement and Miracles," chapter 1, verse 3, in *A Course in Miracles,* p. 9.

8. "The Two Emotions," chapter 13, verse 5, in *A Course in Miracles,* p. 250.

9. "I am sustained by the Love of God," lesson 50 in *A Course in Miracles,* p. 79.

10. Read Tom Carpenter, *The Miracle of Real Forgiveness* (Carpenter Press, 2010). Tom is founder of The Forgiveness Network. Visit the website: www.theforgivenessmovement.org. I also recommend you visit the Facebook page for The Forgiveness Network.

11. Tom Carpenter and Robert Holden, *A Dialogue on Forgiveness,* DVD. Available at www.robertholden.org.

PART II: LOVE IS WHO YOU ARE

1. *Secret beauty.* Read Thomas Merton, *Conjectures of a Guilty Bystander,* ed. Naomi Burton (London: Sheldon Press, 1977), p. 158.

2. *Specialness.* The word *specialness* is used in *A Course in Miracles* to describe the ego's desire to be more, do more, or have more than other egos. It is a competitive mind-set born of the illusion of separation. It is an attempt to be happier than others, but it perpetuates personal suffering.

3. *DSM-IV-TR: Diagnostic and Statistical Manual of Mental Disorders,* 4th rev. ed. (Arlington, VA: American Psychiatric Press, 2000).

4. *Love and stress.* Robert Holden, *Stress Busters* (New York: HarperCollins, 1992), p. 307.

5. John Welwood, *Perfect Love, Imperfect Relationships* (Boston: Shambhala, 2007), p. 12.

6. Gill Edwards, *Wild Love* (London: Piatkus, 2006), p. 168.

Chapter 6: Self-Love Monologue

1. Read the chapter "Awareness Without Evaluating Everything" in Anthony de Mello, *Awareness* (Grand Rapids, MI: Zondervan, 1990).

2. John O'Donohue, *Eternal Echoes* (London: Bantam, 2000), p. 17. For further information on O'Donohue's work, visit his website: www.johnodonohue.com.

Chapter 7: Mirror Exercise

1. Read Eva Wiseman, "Uncomfortable in Our Skin: The Body-Image Report," *The Guardian*, June 10, 2012.

2. Ibid. For a summary of research on body image, visit the Centre for Appearance Research (CAR) online at hls.uwe.ac.uk/research/car.aspx. Also, look at the YMCA work on body image online at www.ymca.co.uk/bodyimage.

3. Disordered Eating has collated statistics from research into anorexia and bulimia in the U.K., the U.S., and the rest of the world. Visit the website: www.disordered-eating.co.uk.

4. Ibid.

5. Read Sarah Boseley, "Self-Harm Practised by One in 12 Adolescents, Study Reveals," *The Guardian*, November 17, 2011; also Paul Moran et al., "The Natural History of Self-Harm from Adolescence to Young Adulthood: A Population-Based Cohort Study," *The Lancet* 379, no. 9812 (January 21, 2012), pp. 236–43.

6. Alain de Botton, *Essays in Love* (London: Picador, 1994), pp. 58–59.

Chapter 8: Childhood Messages

1. "But trailing clouds of glory do we come / From God, who is our home," writes William Wordsworth in *Ode: Intimations of Immortality from Recollections of Early Childhood* (Whitefish, MT: Kessinger Publishing, 2010).

2. For further information, visit www.interfaithfoundation.org.

3. Cheryl Richardson, *The Art of Extreme Self-Care* (Carlsbad, CA: Hay House, 2009). For further information on Cheryl's work, visit her website: www.cherylrichardson.com.

Chapter 9: Your Love Story

1. John Steinbeck, *East of Eden* (New York: Penguin Classics, 2000), p. 268.

2. *Primal lie.* This is the name that Sondra Ray gives to a basic fear and judgment we have about ourselves.

3. Macrina Wiederkehr, *Seasons of Your Heart: Prayers and Reflections* (New York: HarperCollins, 1991).

PART III: LOVE HAS NO CONDITIONS

1. *Alternatives, Piccadilly.* For information, visit www.alternatives.org.uk.

Chapter 10: Is This Love?

1. *J. Krishnamurti and love.* J. Krishnamurti, *Think on These Things* (San Francisco: HarperSanFrancisco, 1997). Also, visit www.jkrishnamurti.org.

2. Read James Baldwin, *Go Tell It on the Mountain* (New York: Penguin Modern Classics, 2001).

3. Hafiz, "The Sun Never Says," in *The Gift,* trans. Daniel Ladinsky (New York: Penguin, 1999), p. 34.

4. "The Needless Sacrifice," chapter 15, verse 7, in *A Course in Miracles.*

5. *Egoism à deux.* A term used by Erich Fromm in *The Art of Loving* (New York: HarperPerennial, 2000), p. 81.

6. Ken Keyes, Jr., *The Power of Unconditional Love* (Coos Bay, OR: Love Line Books, 1990), p. 48.

Chapter 11: I Love You

1. *"I Love You" Inquiry on Facebook.* See May 21, 2012, on my Facebook timeline: www.facebook.com/drrobertholden.

2. Robert A. Johnson, *WE: Understanding the Psychology of Human Love* (San Francisco: HarperSanFrancisco, 1998), p. 189.

3. The Brihadaranyaka Upanishad, in Juan Mascaró, trans., *The Upanishads* (New York: Penguin, 2005), pp. 130–31.

4. *Less than five seconds.* Actually, we may even fall in love in one-fifth of a second, according to research by Syracuse University professor Stephanie Ortigue. See Ortigue et al., "The Neuroimaging of Love," *Journal of Sexual Medicine* 7, no. 11 (November 2010), pp. 3541–52.

5. *Martin Buber and love.* Martin Buber, *I and Thou* (Eastford, CT: Martino Fine Books, 2010), p. 11.

6. Inspired by Ubuntu philosophy. I wrote about this in *Authentic Success,* formerly entitled *Success Intelligence* (Carlsbad, CA: Hay House, 2011), pp. 313–15.

7. Quoted in Kim Phuc, *LOVE: Moments, Intimacy, Laughter, Kinship* (Auckland: M.I.L.K. Publications, 2002), p. 127.

8. Recommended reading: Carl R. Rogers, *A Way of Being* (New York: Houghton Mifflin, 1996).

9. David G. Myers, *Psychology: Eighth Edition in Modules* (New York: Worth Publishers, 2006).

10. Carl R. Rogers, *On Becoming a Person* (London: Constable, 2004).

11. A popular lyric sung by many great artists. One of my favorites is "Thank You (falettinme be mice elf agin)," by Sly and the Family Stone, on their album *Greatest Hits*. This song also features in the soundtrack for the movie *Eat, Pray, Love*.

12. "Heralds of Eternity," chapter 20, verse 5, in *A Course in Miracles*.

13. "The Judgment of the Holy Spirit," chapter 12, verse 1, in *A Course in Miracles*.

14. *If-love*. Bernie S. Siegel, M.D., *Love, Medicine and Miracles* (New York: HarperCollins, 1988). In Bernie's introduction to his website, he writes, "I believe that we are here to contribute love to the planet—each of us in our own way": www.berniesiegelmd.com.

15. Thích Nhất Hạnh, *True Love: A Practice for Awakening the Heart* (Boston: Shambhala, 2006), p. 5.

16. Ibid., pp. 6–7.

17. Ibid., p. 6.

Chapter 12: Show Your Love

1. "It Happens All the Time in Heaven," in *The Subject Tonight Is Love: 60 Wild and Sweet Poems of Hafiz*, trans. Daniel Ladinsky (Pumpkin House Press, 1996), p. 45.

2. *Love styles*. Developed by John Lee. Read Lee, *The Colors of Love* (New York: New Press, 1976).

3. *Love types*. Developed by biological anthropologist Helen Fisher. Read Fisher, *Why Him? Why Her? How to Find and Keep Lasting Love* (London: Oneworld Publications, 2011).

4. *Love languages*. Read Gary Chapman, *The Five Love Languages: The Secret to Love That Lasts* (Chicago: Moody Publishers, 2010). Also visit the website: www.5lovelanguages.com.

5. Anna K. B. Lindstrom and Larry A. Samovar, "Cultural Perspectives on Love," paper presented at the annual meeting of the Western Speech Communication Association, Spokane, WA, February 17–21, 1989.

6. Read Susan Hendrick and Clyde Hendrick, "Love," in *Handbook of Positive Psychology,* ed. C. R. Snyder and Shane J. Lopez (New York: Oxford University Press, 2002), pp. 472–84.

7. Recommended reading: R. E. Dinero et al., "The Influence of Family of Origin and Adult Romantic Partners on Romantic Attachment Security," *Journal of Family Psychology* 22, no. 4 (August 2008), pp. 622–32; also Susan Sprecher and Diane Felmlee, "The Influence of Parents and Friends on the Quality and Stability of Romantic Relationships: A Three-Wave Longitudinal Investigation," *Journal of Marriage and Family* 54, no. 4 (November 1992), pp. 888–900.

PART IV: LOVE KNOWS NO FEAR

Chapter 13: The Mirror Principle

1. *Pick up the mirror.* Susan Jeffers, *The Feel the Fear Guide to Lasting Love* (London: Vermilion, 2007), p. 44.

Chapter 14: Love and Fear

1. *Love and fear.* "The Time of Rebirth," chapter 15, verse 10, in *A Course in Miracles,* p. 325.

2. Introduction to chapter 10 in *A Course in Miracles,* p. 181.

3. "The Judgment of the Holy Spirit," chapter 12, verse 1, in *A Course in Miracles,* p. 181.

4. "The Way to Remember God," chapter 12, verse 2, in *A Course in Miracles,* p. 219.

5. "Seeking and Finding," chapter 12, verse 3, in *A Course in Miracles,* p. 223.

6. *Sondra Ray and LRT.* Read Ray, *The Loving Relationships Treasury* (Berkeley, CA: Celestial Arts, 2006). Visit Sondra's website at www.liberationbreathing.com.

Chapter 15: Love Does Not Hurt

1. Chuck Spezzano, *If it Hurts, It Isn't Love* (New York: Marlowe & Co., 2000).

2. Lency Spezzano, *Make Way for Love* (Psychology of Vision Press, 1998).

3. *Psychology of Vision.* Visit the website: www.psychologyofvision.com.

4. Chuck Spezzano, *Awaken the Gods* (Eureka Springs, AR: Wellspring Publications, 1991), p. 126.

5. Ibid., p. 31.

PART V: LOVE IS THE ANSWER

1. *Transfiguration of Christ.* Matthew 17:1–9, Mark 9:2–9, and Luke 9:28–36.

2. John 4:8 (King James Bible).

3. In his poem "I am a child of love," Rumi tells us, "I profess the religion of love, Love is my religion and my faith. My mother is love. My father is love. My prophet is love. My God is love. I am a child of love. I have come only to speak of love." In Rumi, *Fountain of Fire,* trans. Nader Khalili (Tarzana, CA: Burning Gate Press, 1994).

4. Ramana said, "Love is not different from the Self. Love of an object is of an inferior order and cannot endure. Whereas the Self is Love, in other words, God is Love." Quoted in Sri Munagala Venkataramiah, *Talks with Sri Ramana Maharshi* (Nesma Books, 2003), p. 417.

5. "The Closing of the Gap," chapter 29, verse 1, in *A Course in Miracles,* p. 608.

6. "God Is Love," by Marvin Gaye, appears on the album *What's Going On.*

7. Quoted in Miranda Holden, *Boundless Love* (London: Rider, 2002), p. 203.

Chapter 16: Only Love Is Real

1. "The whole world is a marketplace for love," said Attar. Quoted in James Fadiman and Robert Frager, eds., *Essential Sufism* (San Francisco: HarperSanFrancisco, 2000).

2. *Sri Anandamayi Ma.* Visit www.anandamayi.org/books/booksh1.htm.

3. *Matrix of all matter.* From Max Planck, "The Nature of Matter," speech given in Florence, Italy, in 1944.

4. *Consciousness is fundamental.* Read Peter Russell, *From Science to God: A Physicist's Journey into the Mystery of Consciousness* (Novato, CA: New World Library, 2005).

5. From a conversation with Tom. The words "The real nature of your being is to be loving" also appear in *The Miracle of Real Forgiveness,* p. 29.

6. Erwin Schrödinger, "The Oneness of Mind," in Ken Wilber, ed., *Quantum Questions: Mystical Writings of the World's Great Physicists* (Boston: Shambhala, 2001).

7. Visit the website www.successintelligence.com.

8. *Anita Roddick and love.* In Roddick, *Business as Unusual: The Journey of Anita Roddick and the Body Shop* (London: Thorsons, 2000).

9. Holden, *Authentic Success,* p. 127.

10. Coleman Barks, *The Essential Rumi* (New York: HarperOne, 2004), p. 51.

11. From Steve Jobs's speech to graduates at Stanford University's 114th Commencement on June 12, 2005.

12. Holden, *Authentic Success,* p. 128.

13. Raymond Carver's poem "Late Fragment" is inscribed on his tombstone at Ocean View Cemetery in Port Angeles, WA. This poem appears in a collection entitled *A New Path to the Waterfall* (London: The Harvill Press, 1990).

14. "Looking Within," chapter 12, verse 7, in *A Course in Miracles,* p. 231.

Chapter 17: A Call for Love

1. "Forgiveness offers everything I want," lesson 122 in *A Course in Miracles,* p. 217.

2. Carpenter, *The Miracle of Real Forgiveness.*

3. "Love holds no grievances," lesson 68 in *A Course in Miracles,* p. 115.

4. "You have heard that it was said, 'You shall love your neighbor and hate your enemy.' But I say to you, love your enemies, bless those who curse you, do good to those who hate you, and pray for those who spitefully use you and persecute you, that you may be sons of your Father in heaven," said Jesus in Matthew 5:43–46 (Authorized [King James] Version, Cambridge ed.).

5. Read Byron Katie, *Loving What Is* (London: Rider, 2002) and *I Need Your Love—Is That True?* (London: Rider, 2005).

Chapter 18: The Presence of Love

1. Erich Fromm, *The Art of Loving* (New York: HarperPerennial, 2000).

2. Ibid., p. 1.

3. Ibid., p. 123.

4. Ibid.

5. Ibid.

6. Ibid., p. 17.

7. Ibid., p. 9.

8. Quoted in *Waking from Sleep* by Steve Taylor (Carlsbad, CA: Hay House, Inc., 2010), p. 119.

9. Fromm, *The Art of Loving*, p. 9.

10. Recommended reading: Matthew Greenblatt, *The Essential Teachings of Ramana Maharshi: A Visual Journey* (Carlsbad, CA: Inner Directions Publishing, 2006).

11. Recommended reading: Erwin Schrödinger, *Mind and Matter* (Cambridge: Cambridge University Press, 1958).

12. Fromm, *The Art of Loving*, p. 43.

13. Ibid.

14. Hafiz, "I Know the Way You Can Get," in *I Heard God Laughing*, trans. Daniel Ladinsky (Walnut Creek, CA: Sufism Reoriented, 1996).

15. Recommended reading: Sharon Salzberg, *Lovingkindness: The Revolutionary Art of Happiness* (Boston: Shambhala, 2002).

16. Quoted in Holden, *Boundless Love*, p. 193.

17. *Heart resonance.* See the work of HeartMath at www.heartmath.com; also the Global Coherence Initiative at www.glcoherence.org.

18. *Three degrees of separation.* For an excellent summary, read David Hamilton, "Is Kindness Contagious?", chapter 15 in *The Contagious Power of Thinking* (Carlsbad, CA: Hay House, 2011), pp. 191–99.

19. *Ronny Edry and The Peace Factory.* Visit the website www.israelovesiran.com.

♥ About the Author ♥

Robert Holden, Ph.D., is the creator of the Loveability program. His work on psychology and spirituality has been featured on *Oprah* and *Good Morning America,* and a PBS show called "Shift Happens." He has also been in two major BBC-TV documentaries, *The Happiness Formula* and *How to Be Happy.* His corporate clients include Dove and its Campaign for Real Beauty. He is the author of *Happiness NOW!, Shift Happens!, Authentic Success* (formerly titled *Success Intelligence*), and *Be Happy.* Robert hosts a weekly show on Hay House Radio called *Shift Happens!* He also contributes daily to his Facebook page at www.facebook.com/drrobertholden. For information, visit www.robertholden.org.

❤ The Loveability Program ❤

Robert Holden presents an annual program of public talks and workshops on love, including the three-day signature course called Loveability as well as Love and the Enneagram, Love and Fear (based on the teachings of *A Course in Miracles*), and Love's Philosophy (inspired by poets like Shelley, Rumi, and Hafiz).

Robert has also recorded a series of interviews for Loveability, which features conversations about love with teachers such as Tom Carpenter, Chuck Spezzano, Sharon Salzberg, Marianne Williamson, David Hamilton, Louise Hay, Andrew Harvey, Cheryl Richardson, and others.

For information, visit www.robertholden.org.